GUIDE TO
BRITISH
TOPOGRAPHICAL
PRINTS

GUIDE TO BRITISH TOPOGRAPHICAL PRINTS

RONALD RUSSELL

DAVID & CHARLES

NEWTON ABBOT   LONDON   NORTH POMFRET (VT)

British Library Cataloguing in Publication Data

Russell, Ronald
    Guide to British topographical prints.
    1. Prints, British
    2. Great Britain in art
    I. Title
    769'.4'994107   NE628.2

    ISBN 0-7153-7810-4

Set in 12 on 13pt Bembo
by Ronset Limited, Darwen, Lancashire
and printed in Great Britain by
Biddles Ltd, Martyr Road, Guildford
for David & Charles (Publishers) Limited
Brunel House Newton Abbot Devon

Published in the United States of America
by David & Charles Inc
North Pomfret Vermont 05053 USA

CONTENTS

PLATES

INTRODUCTION

The story of British topographical prints in the eighteenth and nineteenth centuries is a story of change in both techniques and taste. Topography is the study of places, and in this book we are concerned with the pictorial representation of such places as towns, districts, parts of the countryside and buildings in their setting. The print is a reproduction of a design incised into a metal plate by one of a number of methods, or engraved on a block of wood or drawn on a slab of stone or zinc. Any print made by one of these methods is an 'original print'. It was estimated that about 900,000 impressions were taken off one of Thomas Bewick's wood blocks, and although the block must have needed some repair and recutting during its lifetime every one of these impressions can be described as 'original'. What are not original are photographic reproductions of prints, such as have to be used for the illustrations to this book.

To borrow the words of Arthur Hayden, author of one of the most popular of the early twentieth-century studies of the subject, 'it is not the intention of the writer in this introductory chapter to enter into the technique of each class of engraving'. While an understanding of techniques is vital to an appreciation of the subject, it is perhaps better to treat this separately as reference material rather than as part of the narrative. There is a narrative—there is a story to be told; but there are many different ways of telling it. The way that I have chosen is to devote a chapter to each of the major print-making processes in turn. These processes include line engraving on copper, line engraving on steel, aquatint and lithography (taken together), wood engraving and etching. There are also brief surveys of the theory and practice of the 'Picturesque' and of what has been called 'the Turner Print Industry'. Then comes the section on techniques and, finally, annotated lists of artists, engravers, books and other sources of prints. The illustrations have been chosen to represent as wide a range as possible of topographical prints that are not confined to museum or gallery collections but can still be purchased for ready money from a well-stocked print-dealer's shop. Most of the originals are black and white, a few are in sepia (which presents no problems) and a few in colour. The coloured originals—some of the aquatints and a few tinted lithographs—have been reproduced here in black and white because so often the attempt to reproduce them in colour by modern processes does them only injustice. The Daniell aquatints exemplify this; no attempt to reproduce them in colour has been particularly successful. Similar problems arise with the mezzotints of Turner's *Liber Studiorum*. Although these were originally printed in sepia, so subtle are the tonal gradations that reproduction over-emphasises the composition and frustrates the artist's, and the engraver's, intention. On the other hand, most copper and steel engravings, and soft-ground etchings, reproduce quite well.

Topographical prints appeal to a very wide range of interests. Social historians find them useful and sometimes invaluable as visual evidence of places and periods under study. They may at times be the only evidence available but, as we shall see later, caution in interpreting them is often needed. For many people prints are the only contact they have with the graphic arts, if we exclude photography. Many prints are works of art in their own right. Sometimes the artist is also the etcher or engraver—as, for instance, Wenceslaus Hollar—but this is not generally the case. For examples of interpretations see some of Miller's and Varrall's brilliant engravings after Turner, or R. G. Reeve's aquatints of the Thames views of William Westall and Samuel Owen. Prints made many publishers rich, and a few bankrupt; they often popularised the artist who produced the original and even provided his main source of income. In the nineteenth century the sale of the engraving rights sometimes brought the painter more money than the sale of the picture itself. Prints were, and are, collectors' items, decorative souvenirs, and an investment; and the hand-colouring of black and white original impressions is one of the few cottage industries still flourishing today.

Let us look more closely at our definition of topographical prints. The general history of prints in England shows that topography as a subject emerged comparatively late. At the end of the fifteenth century woodcuts were used to illustrate *The Canterbury Tales* and Caxton and his successors built up their own collections of blocks for use in their books. Line-engraved portraits and anatomical studies began to appear in England towards the middle of the sixteenth century and in the following decades engravings of symbolic and allegorical figures adorned the title-pages of many volumes. But throughout this time England was trailing behind the general European achievement in the production of good engraved work. The great masters of the arts of engraving and etching, Dürer, Rembrandt, Callot, had no English equivalents, and the first etcher of real distinction to work in England was the expatriate Wenceslaus Hollar.

It is Hollar who brings us to a major problem of definition; the distinction between landscape and topography. But it is a problem which I suggest we side-step rather than try, possibly in vain, to solve. After all, this is what the great auction houses do; their sale catalogues distinguish between Fine Prints, Decorative Prints, Sporting Prints, Satirical Prints and Topographical Prints, but they do not seem to deal with Landscape Prints. It is also true that they sometimes sell Good English Prints but never Bad English Prints, although there are plenty of the latter to be found. But for the purpose of this Guide, we do not need to trouble too much with this distinction. The prints that we are concerned with are those which represent places, usually taken from a watercolour original or a pencil or chalk drawing made specifically for the purpose. One of the best known of English prints is William Woollett's copper engraving of 'The Destruction of the Children of Niobe', from an oil painting by Richard Wilson. Much of the interest in the painting lies in its dramatic representation of the landscape. Woollett's work on the plate is superb and was widely admired in his own time; he is a major figure in the history of engraving. This is a fine print, but not a topographical one. Similarly an engraving after Turner's 'Hannibal Crossing the Alps' cannot be regarded as topography; but an engraving after Turner's 'Norham Castle' certainly can.

Topography is often regarded as a sort of poor relation of landscape. Until comparatively recently, landscape itself was thought of as a poor relation: 'A History is preferable to a Landscape, Sea-piece, Animals, Fruit, Flowers, or any other Still-Life, pieces of Drollery, &c.', wrote Jonathan Richardson in 1719, 'the reason is . . . they cannot Improve the Mind, they excite no Noble Sentiments . . .' Gradually landscape edged in, as background to portraits and conversation pieces. 'I'm sick of Portraits', wrote Gainsborough in a letter, and in another letter, to a friend in Derbyshire, he elaborated further: 'If the People with their damn'd Faces could but let me alone a little I believe I should soon appear in a more tolerable light . . . I suppose your Country is very woody —pray have your Rocks and Waterfalls! for I am as fond of Landskip as ever.' Henry Fuseli, Keeper of the Royal Academy and Professor of Painting at the beginning of the nineteenth century, could accept the landscapes of Titian, Mola, Salvator, the Poussins, Claude, Elzheimer, Rembrandt and Wilson because 'to them nature disclosed her bosom in the varied light of rising, meridian, setting suns', and in their paintings 'we tread on classic or romantic ground.' But he rejected 'that kind of landscape which is entirely occupied with the tame delineation of a given spot ... what is commonly called Views.' These views, he considered, might please the owners of the acres depicted, and the inhabitants, the antiquary or the traveller, 'but to every other eye they are little more than topography'. Even the two great champions of landscape painting in the mid-nineteenth century, Ruskin (in theory) and Constable (in practice), did not see eye to eye; or at least Ruskin, in his advocacy of Turner, could not see with Constable's eye, asserting that Constable was unable to grasp the meaning of nature. But let the observer judge for himself, only bearing in mind a single sentence from one of Constable's letters: 'My limited and abstracted art is to be found under every hedge and in every lane, and therefore nobody thinks it worth picking up; but I have my admirers, each of whom I consider an host.'

By the middle of the nineteenth century, of course, the battle was won. *The Landscape Painters of England* is the title of a collection of engravings by Louis Marvy, a refugee from the 1848 revolution in France and a friend of W. M. Thackeray, who wrote the comments on the plates. 'There are no incidents in our show upon which the showman can dilate', wrote Thackeray in his preface, 'in most cases he has to introduce his audience to the sight of a simple and quiet landscape, over which ideal pleasure is ever the best commentary, and concerning which it is as hard to explain one's own emotions, as to cause another to share in them ...' The painters represented are Sir Alexander Callcott (placed first because of his title), Turner, Holland, Danby, Creswick, Collins, Redgrave, Lee, Cattermole, W. J. Muller, Harding, Nasmyth, Richard Wilson, E. W. Cooke, Constable, Peter de Wint, David Cox, Gainsborough, David Roberts and Clarkson Stanfield. They make a good team, taken all in all; and when you study a collection such as this, the dividing line between landscape and topography seems irrelevant.

But life was seldom easy, in financial terms, for the landscape artist, despite the rise to respectability of this kind of painting. Sir Edwin Landseer's fortune, mainly gained from selling the copyrights of his pictures, totalled £160,000; but, in a letter about the tribulations of a landscape painter's life, Constable wrote, 'the field of Waterloo is a field of mercy to ours'. Crome's life was a struggle and Cotman died poor. On the whole, the artists who made money in their lifetime were—Turner excepted—the subject painters and the portraitists. Few engravers died rich men.

It is time now to return to the prints themselves, to the contents of the well-stocked print-dealer's shop. Where do the prints come from? Very many of them came from books of travel and topography. They were often specially commissioned to accompany a text; sometimes it was the other way around, with the text being commissioned to accompany the plates. Extra impressions from the plates could be taken and sold separately. Many were issued in instalments, a few prints and pages of text appearing monthly and being collected into volumes when the issue was completed. Sometimes it was not completed, as with Turner's *Picturesque Views in England and Wales* for which 120 subjects were planned but only 96 published when Charles Heath, the publisher at the time, went bankrupt. Occasionally, owners of country houses contributed to the cost of having their estate drawn and engraved, and perhaps the plate would be dedicated to them in return. Some painters—Gainsborough and Cotman among them—made their own etchings to multiply their work, while others sold their copyrights to dealers who employed the engravers and collected the profits. With the major publishers of the late eighteenth and early nineteenth centuries, such as the Boydells and Ackermann, the trade in prints developed vastly; it won John Boydell a fortune, enabled him to become Lord Mayor of London—and then bankrupted him. From Ackermann's Repository in its great years came an enormous number of coloured prints, some as illustrations to splendid publications such as the *Microcosm of London, Oxford* and *Cambridge*, and some—very many—for the *Repository of the Arts* magazine, begun in 1809 as a rival to the long-established *Gentleman's Magazine*, which itself was illustrated by copper engravings. The discovery of lithography and the development of engraving on steel enabled print runs to be increased, although until the process of electrotyping was introduced in about 1850 it was still necessary for all illustrations, except from wood blocks, to be printed separately.

A great number of prints, then, come from books; either directly, with the book being broken up to extract them, or indirectly, as additional impressions or from instalments. Many antiquarian booksellers carry a stock of prints which have been taken from damaged or incomplete volumes, or perhaps even from volumes bought specifically for breaking up. Complete illustrated topographical books are becoming very expensive and difficult to find. Those that are more frequently met with—the tours of Gilpin and Pennant, for example—usually have illustrations that are less acceptable without their text. Gilpin's aquatints make sense in their context but mounted and framed they can hardly have a wide appeal. They have no particular topographical relevance and were not intended to have any.

Generally, the practice of most dealers and keepers of collections is to classify topographical prints according to the geographical area represented, rather than by the name of the artist, although this is not always done with some of the better known or better quality series. One must ask to see the prints of a particular county or town, or to see the Bucks, Sandbys or Daniells. The print itself usually carries certain information. On the left, below the engraved surface, you will find the name of the original artist and on the right the name of the engraver. In the centre is the name of the subject and below that sometimes you will find the publisher's name and the date. In most instances the date is that of the first published issue; the print you are examining may come from a later run. If the print is one of a series, there may be a number above the printed surface, usually on the right-hand side. With engravings, all this is contained within the plate-mark, the recession in the paper made by the printing process. Some prints have been trimmed within the plate-mark, to suit the page size of a book or possibly for purposes of framing. With wood engravings and lithographs there is no plate-mark. Many wood engravings give no indication of the artist or designer. Lithographs, on the other hand, are usually quite informative, often stating who made the original drawing, who transferred it to the stone and who printed and published the finished product. What lithographs frequently omit, however, is the date. The amount of information obtained directly from a print, therefore, varies considerably. Take a few of the plates used in this Guide. The illustration of the 'Mill at Peter Tavy' tells us that the mill is the property of the Revd E. A. Bray, that the plate was drawn, engraved and published by F. C. Lewis, 1843, and that the original picture is in the collection of T. Webster, Esq. We are not told whether the plate appeared in a book but, as it is a Devonshire scene, we can look it up in a catalogue and guide compiled by Mr J. V. Somers Cocks, *Devon Topographical Prints, 1660-1870*, published in 1977. Devon is the only county fortunate enough to have such a thorough record; without this we might have to search through a number of reference books or consult the print room of one of the larger galleries or museums. Another informative plate is the 'View of the Floating Dock, Bristol'. This gives the name of the artist, W. H. Bartlett, and of the etcher, J. C. Varrall, identifies certain landmarks, is dedicated to the City Chamberlain, tells us the date of publication, 1 March 1830, the name of the publisher, Longman & Co, Paternoster Row, and the name of the printer, Barnett & Son. It also announces that it was 'For Britton's Picturesque Antiquities of English Cities'. The plates for many of the publications with which John Britton was associated have a convenient way of declaring themselves; 'For the Beauties of England & Wales' is met with frequently.

But some prints tell you very little. The lithograph of Hyde Park Corner tells you nothing about itself, the information being in the volume from which it was taken: *Original Views of London As It Is* by Thomas Shotter Boys. Sometimes Boys did put his own name into his pictures, on the back of a cart or on the sign over a shop. In this example he did not do so; not that it matters, as his style is unmistakable. The view of 'New Market', however, presents a greater problem. There is no indication of artist or engraver, only the statement 'Published by J. Mawman, London, January 1st, 1821'. It is a sepia-tinted aquatint, but for 1821 the style seems decidedly odd. So how do you find out more about it? Here you would have to consult an expert, as this particular print is something of a freak. It is one of the aquatints from a translation of an Italian manuscript of the *Travels of Cosmo the Third through England in 1669*. The original drawings were made at that time—hence their style—and deposited in the Laurentian Library in Florence. These drawings were copied and were eventually passed on to the London illustrator, Thomas Hosmer Shepherd, to prepare for aquatinting. And here I must acknowledge that some of this information comes from Abbey's *Scenery* (see bibliography) and the rest from J. F. C. Phillips' recent study *Shepherd's London*, in which another of these prints is reproduced. Fortunately it is seldom that you come across anything quite so complicated as this. With copper engravings, some of the least informative prints come from the publications of Alexander Hogg in the later eighteenth century, many of which tell you nothing except the name of the place depicted. But as Hogg was prosecuted for using engravings which had appeared in other publishers' books, this reticence is understandable.

It is necessary here to say something briefly about 'states' and 'proofs', which especially concern copper engravings and etchings. Strictly, a proof is an impression taken while the work is in progress to see how it is getting on. With a copper plate, the best impressions are the earliest as the plate quickly wears. These first impressions might be run off on fine paper—India or Japan paper—and sold at a far higher price than the later ones. Often these are called 'proofs' or 'artist's proofs' and they may be signed or numbered. Turner was notorious for demanding an excessive number of proofs for himself, which displeased his publishers, and the engraver John Pye said that the woman who stitched the *Liber* prints together was paid in proofs instead of money, which she sold to buy food.

'States' have been defined as 'the different stages through which a plate passes in the course of its history'. For example, a number of impressions are taken by the printer from the finished plate before any lettering is added—these are the first state. Some lettering is added—perhaps open lettering—and more impressions taken—the second state. The lettering may be changed or corrected—some mistakes never seem to have been corrected, such as the description of the engraving of Monnow Bridge after Gastineau as 'Ragland'

—and impressions taken again—the third state. Or alterations may be made to the plate itself, or it may have to be repaired, so more states appear. Except to the connoisseur or the really high-powered collector, none of this is normally very important. Arthur Hayden, noting the great differences in price demanded for varying states of a particular print, where the only visible difference is the presence or absence of a couple of dots before or after the printer's name, observes that 'to collect prints in such a fashion is to reduce the subject to the level of stamp-collecting, where the misprint of a careless official means pounds added to the value, where dots and perforations and grains more mucilage at the back are added worth to the philatelist'.

What is important is the condition of the print itself, and the ability to recognise an impression which is what it says it is and not the result of somebody's working over the worn-out plate of an engraver and passing it off as the original engraver's work. The chapter on Turner has a little to say about what happened to some of his plates in later years, and he was by no means the only artist to have his work misrepresented after his death. The development of engraving on steel, and the steel-facing of copper plates, put an end to this type of misrepresentation—or defacing as it might be more appropriate to call it. It also put an end to the financial manoeuvring over proofs and states, which at times descended to deliberate faking, as several thousand impressions could be taken off a steel plate without any detectable deterioration of quality. It was really only in the more limited field of pure etching that proofs and states continued to matter.

Now we come to the question of colouring. Nearly all topographical line engraving was originally issued uncoloured but it is becoming progressively more difficult to find prints in that condition. With an engraving or an etching, the 'colour' is simply the colour of the ink used to print it. The description often found, 'an original print hand-coloured', means that the black and white impression has been watercoloured by someone unconnected with its original manufacture: as I said before, hand-colouring is one of the few cottage industries left. Sometimes it is done tactfully and delicately; and sometimes the result is hideous. Of course it adds to the cost of the print, but while the demand is there the dealers will see that it is met.

Aquatints are a different matter. By no means all aquatints were coloured, but those that were, were coloured as part of the original production process. Some were printed in sepia ink, like those illustrating Samuel Ireland's books on the Thames and the Wye, F. C. Lewis's *Scenery of the Dart*, and the *Cosmo* plates already mentioned. There is an issue of Ireland's *Wye* with green tones added to the sepia. The fully coloured aquatints were printed in coloured ink—

two different coloured inks were sometimes used—and finished by hand before the plates were published. The basic tones, usually browns, greens or blues, predominate, with the touches of brighter colour catching the eye. Good coloured aquatints closely resemble watercolours and are sometimes mistaken for them. Very rarely you may come across a copy of a book with aquatints in more than one state—basic uncoloured and fully coloured versions perhaps. There are a few scarce drawing books—*A Treatise on Landscape Painting and Effect in Water Colours*, first edition 1814, by David Cox, is one of the best examples—which contain aquatint views both plain and coloured. The coloured examples show how successfully aquatint could achieve the effect of watercolour.

With lithography, colour moved in gradually. Uncoloured lithographs could be coloured by hand before publication. Two stones could be used, one of which was tinted; then the lithotint process was developed, notably by James Duffield Harding. Working with the printer Hullmandel, Thomas Shotter Boys produced a superb set of chromolithographs of architectural views in several European cities in which four or five stones were used for each plate. For later chromolithographs, double this number of stones were used, but obviously this was not a process that could be extended indefinitely. For the 300 chromolithographs in J. B. Waring's *Masterpieces of Industrial Art and Sculpture at the International Exhibition*, 1862, no fewer than 3,000 lithographic stones were used; Waring himself claimed that it would have taken one artist, working alone, 42 years to prepare them. What is even more significant is that the plates were from photographs 'supplied by the London Photographic and Stereoscopic Company', and this particular book was described as 'the finest and the last of this class of volume'.

The application of colour to prints, then, is either by hand, before or after publication, or by mechanical or semi-mechanical means as part of the printing process. According to circumstances, the artist may or may not have control over the colouring process. William Daniell and Thomas Shotter Boys are two artists who did, in different ways, have this control. Daniell was not only painter and engraver but also co-publisher of his British topographical plates, and Boys claimed that he himself originated and invented the method by which his chromolithographs were produced. But in other instances the colouring may be quite arbitrary, determined by the printer or one of his employees, or by a colourist employed by a dealer in prints. Comparatively little line engraving was printed in colour; many stipple-engraved plates were, but this method was hardly ever used for topography. Coloured woodcuts could be produced by using several blocks but again this method was very rarely employed in

British topography. The brightly coloured small prints made in the mid-nineteenth century by George Baxter, which he called his 'oil pictures', and which were specially intended for ladies' scrap-books, are outside the area of this Guide, being mostly subject pictures with no topographical relevance. An artist of major stature who also falls outside the bounds of this survey is William Blake, who experimented widely with different methods of colour printing, line engraving, wood engraving and etching, but whose interests lay in other directions than representations of scenery and views.

One important method of printmaking—the mezzotint—also has little relevance to our topic. This was developed in England in the later years of the seventeenth century, when the leading practitioners included Francis Place, John Smith and George White. In the following decades little work of note was produced; then in the 1750s there was a marked revival in mezzotinting with James MacArdell's many plates after the portraits of Reynolds, and fine prints being produced by William Pether, Valentine Green, James Walker, John Raphael Smith and many others. Mezzotint, in which the engraver works from a black ground to light, is well suited to portraits and to subject pictures but generally is seldom appropriate for representing topographical views. It was, however, used for the making of two major series of prints. The first was Turner's *Liber Studiorum* of which all the plates except the first were in mezzotint. The same process, this time on a steel instead of copper ground, was also used for the *River Scenery* plates in the late 1820s.

The second series is *Various Subjects of Landscape, Characteristic of English Scenery*—after paintings by John Constable—usually known as *English Landscape Scenery*, a set of 22 plates by David Lucas issued in parts between 1830 and 1832. Constable intended this publication, to which he contributed an explanatory text, both to summarise his work and to widen its understanding and appreciation among the public at large. In it he tries to express 'the chiaroscuro of Nature', to mark—as he himself wrote—'the influence of light and shadow upon Landscape', not only in its general effect on the 'whole', and as a means of rendering a proper emphasis on the 'parts', in painting, but also to show its use and power as a medium of expression, so as to note 'the day, the hour, the sunshine, and the shade'. Mezzotint is the most suitable medium in which to express the contrast between light and dark; it is good for drama but not for colour. Like Turner, Constable took enormous trouble over the plates, altering, amending, suggesting, improving; Graham Reynolds says in his biography of Constable, 'it is small wonder that the engraver ended up as a pauper and a drunkard.' As the work continued, the painter became depressed. 'I have thought much on my book', he wrote to Lucas in 1831, 'and all my reflections on the subject go to oppress me—its duration, its expence, its hopelessness of remuneration, all are unfavourable—added to which I now discover that the printsellers "are watching it as their lawfull prey" . . . The expence is too enormous for a work that has nothing but your beautifull feeling and execution to recommend it—the painter himself is totally unpopular and ever will be, on this side of the grave certainly . . .' Few copies were sold in Constable's lifetime, although the plates are masterly and today are in keen demand. In his *English Landscape Scenery* and in Turner's *Liber Studiorum* actual places are depicted, but the virtue of the mezzotint is in its translation of the atmosphere, the contrast of light and shadow; the topography itself is not of first importance, and in some of the plates it is of very little importance at all.

Our survey of topographical prints comes to an end in the 1870s. There are some interesting advertisements in Black's *Guide Book Advertiser* for 1877. They include a bookseller's announcement that W. H. Bartlett's *Scenery and Antiquities of Ireland*, with 119 steel engravings, published at 42 shillings, is being sold at half price. On the following page, J. Valentine of Dundee advertises 'Photographs of Scottish Scenery, embracing a very large series of the principal places of interest in the Lowlands and Highlands.' The advertisement includes a letter to Valentine from the late Earl of Dalhousie: 'Sir, I think it due to you, as an artist, to inform you that I had the honour of presenting the set of your Photographs to the Queen, and that Her Majesty was pleased to express her approval of them as works of art.' Selections of photographs made up in various bindings, including Clan Tartan Wood, cost from one to ten guineas. On another page G. W. Wilson & Co of Aberdeen advertise 'the largest selection of Photographs of Scottish Scenery' at similar prices, these photographs being 'sold by all respectable Booksellers and Printsellers, and by Agents in every district which the Views illustrate'. The age of engraved topography was drawing rapidly to a close.

The last of the old methods to compete for a time with photography in the commercial sphere was wood engraving. Being cheap and easy to print from, the wood block continued to be used in magazines, guides and popular books into the twentieth century. There was also something of a revival of wood engraving by artists of note, especially for limited editions of books. Etching and, a few years later, lithography also became the concern of a number of artists. What is known as 'the etching revival' was headed by J. Whistler and Seymour Haden who for many aspirants reopened the artistic possibilities of this mode of expression. Whistler also took up lithography, moving it firmly from the world of commerce to the world of art.

But it is arguable that the finest work was done when commerce and art together combined. 'In the first part of the nineteenth century', wrote William Ivins in 1953, 'the techniques of etching and of mixed etching and engraving, especially at the hands of such men as reproduced the drawings and paintings of Turner, were carried to such a state of technical surety and expertness as had never before and has not since been equalled.' John Sell Cotman, Hogarth and the Finden brothers are among the few whom Ivins names as excelling in this respect. In a well-known passage from a lecture he gave in 1853, Ruskin criticised those who spent money on engravings instead of buying paintings, declaring that they were paying a man for sitting for hours 'at a dirty table in a dirty room' sniffing nitric acid and, using a magnifying glass, cutting on a steel plate 'certain notches and scratches of which the effect is to be the copy of another man's work'. And what about the engraver's case? John Pye, an engraver after Turner, gained international recognition for the quality of his work. For one publication alone, Peacock's *Polite Repository*, an annual pocket book, he said he had engraved over a thousand plates. He described much of this work as 'making a silk purse out of a sow's ear', but excepted the designs of William Havell, recognising in him an artist of worth. Born in 1782, three years before the death of William Woollett who set a new standard for copper engraving in England, Pye died in 1874 at the end of the era. Woollett himself was born in 1735. Within the lifespans of those two men, each of whom was a leading contributor, an extraordinary amount of superb work was completed.

Earlier in this chapter I said that for some people prints were investment possibilities. Arthur Hayden in 1906 described aquatint as 'a somewhat neglected field' and mentioned that a complete bound set of Daniell's *Voyage around Great Britain* could be bought for about 25 guineas. This set when first collected and published cost £60 in the ordinary edition and £90 on thick paper. In 1978 a set sold at auction for £7,600 and some of the individual plates are now priced at almost four times Hayden's quotation for the whole set of 308. Topographical prints are now in far greater demand than they were even a few years ago, while stipple engravings, which fetched high prices early this century, are less regarded.

But any price guide to prints is bound to be misleading. One can give only the most general indication. Good impressions of rare copper engravings and fine coloured aquatints are towards the top of the market, as are some lithographs, both coloured and tinted. Uncoloured aquatints, the majority of lithographs and large series of engravings, such as those by Johannes Kip, come next. Steel engravings are at the lower end of the market, together with the poorer examples of copper engravings. The condition of the print, its degree of rarity and its subject are all highly relevant. One print from a series may cost four times as much as another in equally good condition simply because of the subject depicted; this is very evident in the larger series such as Arnout's coloured lithographs, Kip's views of country houses, Ackermann's *Oxford* and *Cambridge*, and Daniell's *Voyage*. And a print of, say, Canterbury bought in Canterbury is likely to cost you more than if you bought it in Yorkshire; on the other hand, you might not be able to find it in Yorkshire at all, so things tend to even themselves out. London is the best hunting ground, as might be expected, and there are regular auctions of prints at the larger auction houses. But there are many excellent dealers outside London; the best advice is to seek and, with luck, you may find.

Etchings are rather different. Many print-dealers do not stock them; they may be handled by specialists and sometimes can be found alongside water-colours. They are more likely to be classified under the name of the artist than by subject. Prices are affected by states and the presence or absence, in more recent items, of signatures. With etchings—and the same applies to other types of print—until you feel you really know the subject you can do no better than find a dealer you can trust and take his advice. And don't buy anything that gives you the slightest feeling of uneasiness or that you do not really like.

Build up your experience of prints by examining collections in museums and galleries. Towards the end of this Guide you will find lists of books illustrated by topographical prints. Most of these books are valuable; some can be found in major libraries and many titles occur in the lists of antiquarian booksellers. Prices are rising all the time: J. C. Bourne's *Great Western Railway* was offered at £350 in 1969 and at £2,450 nine years later. In the same period, Hassell's *Tour of the Grand Junction* rose from £55 to £490. Try to see as many of these books as you can; handle them carefully and examine them closely. In this way you will learn a great deal about the different types of topographical prints, their characters and their qualities. Then you are less likely to confuse modern reproductions with the genuine article, to be fooled by fakes or fobbed off with poor or late impressions for an exorbitant price. Not that this is common practice today. Evidence indicates that the print market has far more integrity now than ever before; the confusion is more likely to arise from ignorance than from deliberate dishonesty. There is every likelihood that you will get the fairest of deals from your sellers of prints or antiquarian books, almost all of whom are enthusiasts and willing to share their enthusiasms and knowledge with you.

Let me end this chapter with a tribute to the engravers, etchers and litho-graphers of this period, who worked so hard to give so much visual pleasure to so many people, often for very little financial return.

EARLY ETCHING, AND LINE ENGRAVING ON COPPER

The first artist to devote himself extensively—though not entirely—to British topography was Wenceslaus Hollar. He was born in Prague in 1607, learnt etching in Germany, and in 1636 was brought to England by Thomas Howard, Earl of Arundel, for whom he worked until Howard's death ten years later. During that time he etched copies from the Earl's collection of paintings and drawings and also made some plates from his own studies of Greenwich, Richmond and various London scenes. Between 1644 and 1652 Hollar lived in Antwerp, where he etched from drawings he had made previously in England, including the views of Arundel's estate at Albury.

After his patron died, Hollar worked mostly for publishers and printsellers. The engraver William Faithorne, who had a print shop in London, employed him, and among the books he illustrated was Dugdale's *History of St Paul's*. He also etched impressive plates of London before and after the Great Fire of 1666, but despite his industry—he produced in his lifetime more than 2,500 plates— he never made much money. Horace Walpole wrote of him: 'To have passed a long life in adversity, without the errors to which many men of genius have owed it, and to have ended that life in destitution of common comforts, merely from the insufficient emoluments of a profession, and with a strictly moral character, such was the fate of Hollar!' It was said that as he lay dying on 28 March 1677, bailiffs broke in to seize his bed, the only piece of furniture he had left.

Costume and portraits were among Hollar's subjects, but it is his topographic work for which he is most notable—careful, perceptive work, freely and rapidly executed and, because he was both draughtsman and etcher, reliable as a record of what he saw. His views have a fluidity of line very different from the rigid formality that was shortly to follow.

Daniel King worked in a similar manner to Hollar and may have learnt the craft of etching from him. About 1670 a sheet of 101 small-scale views by King appeared under the title of *An Orthographical Designe of Severall Views upon Ye Road, in England and Wales*. These were intended to accompany Camden's *Britannia*, the English edition of which was published in 1637, in order 'that where he mentions such places the Curious may see them'. The views themselves are miniatures, arranged in strips, with references on some of them to page numbers in Camden's volume. One strip shows a view of 'Lampton Colliery' in Durham, a very early—if not the earliest—picture of an English industrial site; next to it are some tombstones at Nun Appleton, then 'Robbin hoods well', 'Stones at Burrow', 'St Rob: Chapel' at York, the passage 'from Leverpole to Worel Beston Castle', and Holt Castle in Flintshire. The sheet is an assorted collection of wide-ranging topography, mostly buildings but with a few landscapes included.

It is possible that King died before the *Orthographical Designe* was published; the *Dictionary of National Biography* suggests 1664 as the date of his death. He seems to have worked as an etcher, engraver and publisher, both in Chester and London. He wrote *Miniatura; or the Art of Limning* and published at least two books, one a collection of plates of cathedral and conventual churches, and the other a substantial work, *The Vale-Royall of England*, being a geographical and historical description of the County Palatine of Chester with a section on the Isle of Man. The full title of this book runs to some 150 words. It was published in 1656, King himself contributing about seventeen engravings, and there was also a plan of Chester with an inset prospect by Hollar. William Smith, William Webb, Samuel Lee and James Chaloner wrote the text. King had no reputation as a writer; Sir William Dugdale, for whom he had made some plates, described him as 'an ignorant silly fellow . . . an arrant knave', who could not write a word of true English. *The Vale-Royall* was republished in 1819 as part of George Ormerod's massive *History of the County Palatine and City of Chester*.

One of the best known and best executed sets of late seventeenth-century prints was David Loggan's views of the colleges of Oxford and Cambridge. Born in Danzig, Loggan came to England before he was twenty, gained something of a reputation in London through his drawings and moved to Oxford where he became engraver to the university. His *Oxonia Illustrata* was published in 1675, with 40 large plates; he then began work on a companion collection, *Cantabrigia Illustrata*, published in 1690. These views are notable for their accuracy and sensitivity to detail of both the architecture and the gardens of the colleges. A Dutchman, Michael Burghers, who also moved to

Oxford, probably assisted with some of the Oxford plates; he also engraved many of the early Oxford Almanacks, the plates for one of the very first of the major county natural histories, Dr Robert Plot's *Natural History of Staffordshire*, 1686, and some topographical views for *The Parochial Antiquities of Ambrosden* by White Kennett. Loggan's pupil, Robert White, helped with some of the university engravings and engraved the first of the Almanacks and some architectural plates. He concentrated mostly on portraiture, however, working sometimes directly from life on to the copper plate.

John Lewis Roget, in his authoritative *History of the Old Water-Colour Society*, pointed out that many of the earlier topographers both drew and engraved their subjects, and it is often only the engravings that have survived. He defended them against the charge of producing merely crude works of art and effectively summarised their achievement:

> The fact of an old topographic print's being stiff and devoid of the sensuous charm of beauty need not disentitle it to respect as a characteristic embodiment of the important features of the place or object depicted. The producers of such works were content to describe in the simple graphic language of their day the outward appearance, not only of the objects, but of the people among whom they lived, costumed as they really were, and engaged in their ordinary pursuits . . . No doubt there is enough to despise in our ancestors' conception of the picturesque beauties of the land; but we at least learn from these topographers what were regarded in their time as its prominent features. They indicate, even by their omissions, to what kinds of visible objects public interest was then chiefly confined.

Roget's comments were published in 1891, a time when these early prints were rather less valued than they are today, hence his use of the word 'despise' which would hardly be appropriate to the modern collector. Loggan's work, for example, is in high demand and its prices reflect this.

Roget also showed that much topographic landscape of this period featured buildings and other objects of interest found on old maps and charts. These representations, lacking scale and perspective, often seem amusing to the present-day observer, but they were not intended to be so. Some of the sixteenth- and seventeenth-century maps of Agas, Blaeu and Speed incorporate bird's-eye views of places, and this technique of illustration was developed

Plate 1 (overleaf) Kip's view of Longleat, after Leonard Knyff's drawing, a typical example of the work of these two expatriates

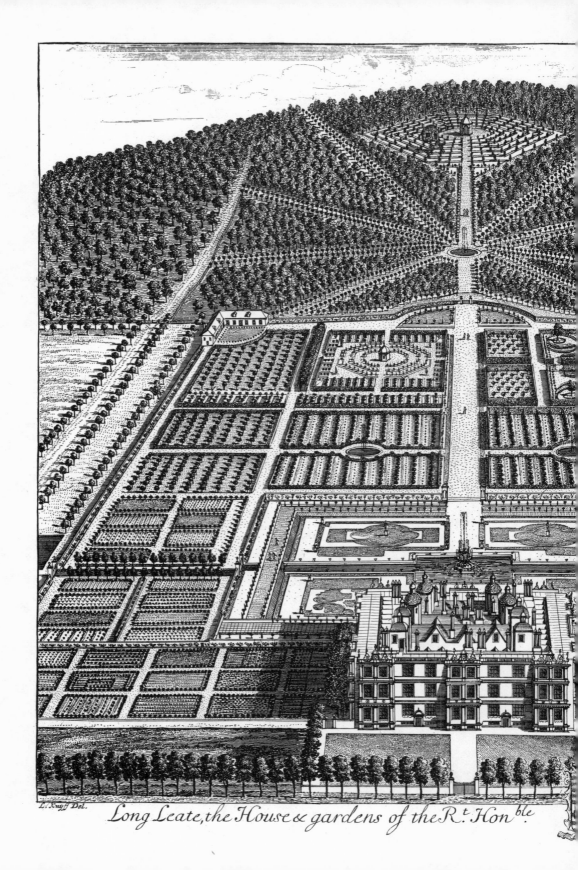

Long Leate, the House & gardens of the R.t Hon.ble

L. Knyff Del.

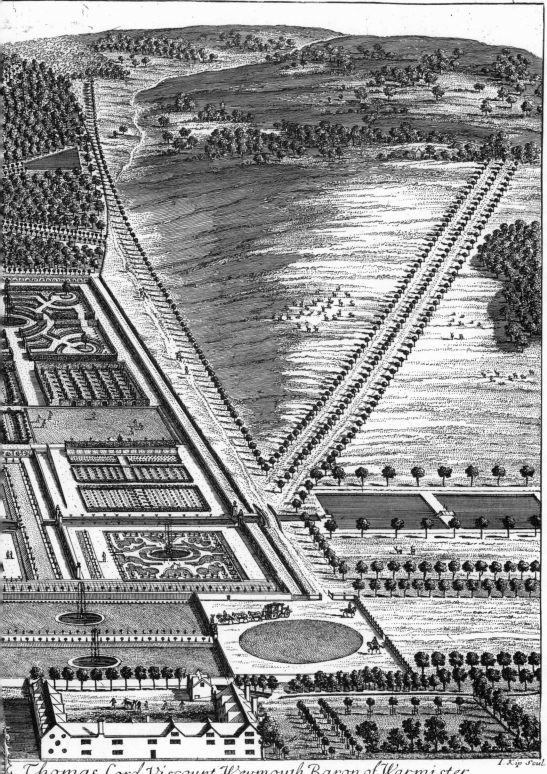

Thomas Lord Viscount Weymouth, Baron of Warmister

I. Kip Scul.

much further in the large number of plates of the *Nouveau Théâtre de la Grande Bretagne*, first published in 1708 and republished with additions in four volumes in subsequent years as *Britannia Illustrata*. Almost all these plates were etched and engraved by Johannes Kip, a Dutchman who emigrated to England in the late 17th century. Most of the earlier plates were after drawings by another Dutchman, Leonard Knyff, while Kip himself drew and engraved the majority of the plates in the second volume. A wider selection of draughtsmen and engravers worked on the last two volumes. Before these two were completed, a note appeared in a reprint of the first two volumes stating that there was a third volume in hand and 'any Gentleman paying Five Guineas towards the Graving, may have their Seat inserted'. The publisher, J. Smith of The Strand, offered the published plates for sale singly, as well as other prints suitable 'for Halls, Parlors, Stair-cases, etc'.

The *Britannia Illustrata* plates are a fairly comprehensive record of the great houses of the time and of their grounds, many of them formally laid out in the Elizabethan style. There is no attempt to portray perspective; figures and trees in the distance are shown the same size as those in the foreground. The sun is shining—occasionally there is a suggestion of a thrown shadow—and a few people stroll about the grounds, singly or in pairs. In the 'Long Leate' plate (Plate 1), seven people appear to be playing a form of cricket or bowls; six horses are drawing a coach around a field which is only twice the length of the complete equipage and through whose minute gate it could not possibly have entered, while two horsemen trot around. Everything is neat and tidy, trim and organised; Viscount Weymouth, the owner of the house, must have been proud of this depiction. These plates are not strictly bird's-eye views, but in them Kip found a method of showing everything in the same degree of detail as if the bird was on two or three different levels simultaneously. Incidentally, to judge by the selection of subjects, Gloucestershire was the county most favoured by the aristocracy of the time. Sir Robert Atkyns' notable book on that county, *The Ancient and Present State of Gloucestershire*, first published 1712, also includes over sixty large plates by Kip; Sir Henry Chauncy's *Historical Antiquities of Hertfordshire*, 1700, was illustrated in a similar way. The two-volume augmented edition of Sir William Dugdale's *Antiquities of Warwickshire Illustrated*, issued in 1730, contained 14 double-page engraved plates as well as many single-page plates and a portrait of the author by Hollar. It was of this book that the antiquarian Gough said, 'it must stand at the head of all our county histories.' The first edition had appeared in 1656, the same year as King's *Vale-Royall of England*.

The increasing interest in topography was also reflected in the subjects chosen to illustrate the annual Oxford Almanacks. The 1677 issue, the third to appear, was engraved by G. Edwards and was the first to show a view of Oxford, although it was merely as a background to an assortment of allegorical figures. Thereafter, apart from an occasional digression in the first two decades, the University Press determined on local topography or architecture as the subject for all succeeding issues. Many of the earlier plates were engraved by Burghers; later in the eighteenth century the Basires, father and son, took over, engraving plates after many major artists including the Rookers, Edward Dayes and J. M. W. Turner.

Kip died in 1722, about the time when the Buck brothers, Samuel and Nathaniel, were beginning their massive undertaking of illustrating 'the venerable remains of above four hundred Castles, Monasteries, Palaces, etc., in England and Wales'. In the next 30 years they produced 420 of these views and nearly a hundred prospects of cities and larger towns. The plates were issued in numbers, which were collected and published by Robert Sayer in 1774 in three volumes. In the earlier prints, as Roget says, 'there is little or no imitation of actual texture. Ruined walls have none of the look of crumbling stone. Edged with fringes of vegetation, neatly trimmed, like whiskers, they are themselves perfectly smooth, as if cut in wood or card, showing marvellous coherence in broken arches and masonry.' As the brothers became more experienced the plates improved with figures appearing and incidents taking place. Many of the prospects are interesting in themselves and have long explanatory captions (Plate 2). The 'South-West Prospect of Birmingham', for example, dated 1731, shows an attractive country town on a hillside, 'neither Borough nor Corporation ... only a Lordship', but nevertheless already famous as a centre of trade.

One of the later plates, the 'North-West Prospect of the University and Town of Cambridge', taken from the gravel pits near Trinity Conduit head, lists thirty places of interest and gives a history of both town and university. The buildings are engraved with a keen eye to accuracy and the foreground is dotted with elegant figures, some in academic dress and one seated on a shooting-stick, conversing with appropriately elegant gestures, but the Bucks hardly bothered at all with the sky. In 1749 the brothers published five large plates of London and Westminster, extending from the 'New Bridge at Westminster' to London Bridge. The Bucks carefully stated where the drawings were made: from Mr Schevas' Sugar House, opposite to York House, Mr Watson's Summer House opposite to Somerset House, Mr Everard's Summer House opposite to St Bride's Church and from the west part of the leads of St Mary Overy's Church in Southwark. As a topographical record of the north bank

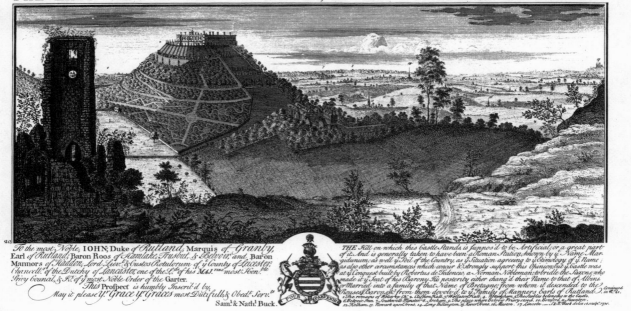

Plate 2 The east view of Belvoir Castle in the county of Leicester, drawn and engraved by Samuel and Nathaniel Buck, 1730. This is from the middle period of the Bucks' Views and is reasonably detailed, with attention drawn in the caption to seventeen features in the view. The plate is dedicated to the Duke of Rutland

of the Thames, the plates leave nothing to be desired.

It seems that the better plates were produced when Nathaniel, the younger brother, was working with Samuel; after Nathaniel's death Samuel continued to exhibit drawings but does not appear to have carried on with engraving. Compared to the work of Hollar—and even of Kip—the Bucks' plates, on the whole, show up poorly; yet they still represent the best topographical engraving of their time. The London print trade was mostly concerned with selling etchings and engravings by foreign craftsmen, sometimes after English portrait originals. When William Hogarth, who learned about engraving while apprenticed to a silversmith, turned to producing illustrations for books and later for his own satirical comments on society, he soon found that others were stealing his designs and selling them on their own account. As the law was powerless to prevent this, Hogarth led a campaign to change the law. In 1735 the Copyright Act was passed, forbidding the copying of a print without permission for a period of 14 years from the original date of publication. A fine of one shilling was to be levied on each illegal impression discovered. This is the Act referred to in the phrase 'published as the Act directs' found on prints subsequent to this date. It took a few years before the stimulus provided by the Act became evident, but by the 1760s the situation had greatly changed. In 1763, at least 49 engravers were known to be at work, one of the best known, and a specialist in landscape, being William Woollett.

Woollett was born in 1735 and was apprenticed to John Tinney, an engraver who also owned a print shop in the Strand. In 1761 he was commissioned by John Boydell, who had recently established himself as a print publisher, to etch and engrave a picture by Richard Wilson, 'The Destruction of the Children of Niobe'. For this Woollett received about £150, more than Wilson was paid for the painting. Selling at five shillings a print, the venture made £2,000 for Boydell, with many of the impressions being sold in France. Woollett, who 'was wont to celebrate the completion of a plate by firing a cannon from the roof of his house', went on to engrave further works by Wilson; he also did Benjamin West's famous 'Death of General Wolfe', as well as several landscapes after George Smith of Chichester. He had a high reputation in his own day, and was appointed Historical Engraver to King George III; but when he died in 1785, from an injury received some years earlier while playing skittles, he left little money for his widow and daughters. Woollett's work may seem rather dark and heavy today but in the history of English landscape engraving he is of major importance.

'During the 1760s', wrote Martin Hardie, 'there arose in this country a school of engravers which was soon equal to any to be found abroad. The leaders of this school swiftly created a new public and it was they and their followers (among whom must be included the artist-engravers such as Paul Sandby) who popularised painting and, in particular, the landscape genre.' Sandby, like Hogarth and the Bucks, was something of an exception—an artist who made his own prints and was therefore recording what he saw as he himself had seen it. Far more often, the engraver was the third or fourth person in the reproductive process. First in the line was the painter or draughtsman, who sketched the view on the spot. Then a draughtsman might work over the sketch for the engraver. Perhaps an etcher was brought in to lay down the groundwork on the plate. Then the engraver, who might never have seen the original drawing, let alone the actual scene, completed the work (Plate 3). Hence we should not be surprised if well-known buildings—like King's College Chapel, Cambridge —seem to have changed in proportion since the eighteenth century. There is a marked difference between the work of men such as Woollett or Sir Robert Strange, who engraved after a carefully finished oil painting, and the work of those whose original may have been a lightly touched pen and wash sketch.

The second half of the eighteenth century saw a remarkable movement in taste, in both landscape and architecture, towards romanticism or 'the Pictures-

Publish'd by W. Darton & J. Harvey London Jan 12. 1805.

Plate 3 'The Engraver', from *Jack of All Trades*, published by Darton and Harvey, London, 1805. Note the looking-glass he is using to reverse the image of the original

que'. This movement applied across the whole range of the arts (see bibliography for some of the more readily accessible material on the subject). Hardie's 'new public' for art was meanwhile growing and had to be satisfied.

Among the first to seize this opportunity was John Boydell, born in 1719, the son of a Derbyshire land surveyor. About 1740 he went to London and became apprenticed to the engraver William Henry Toms who worked on topographical and architectural subjects, including churches and country houses. Soon Boydell began publishing his own views at a shilling each and, having finished his apprenticeship, he set up on his own, bringing out in 1751 a collection of 152 views of England and Wales drawn and engraved by himself. John Pye, himself a leading engraver, wrote of these prints in his *Patronage of British Art*, 1845: 'In the present day such talent as they evince would not enable an artist to live; yet they originated for Mr Boydell the fame and fortune which he acquired.'

Now with some money behind him, Boydell was able to commission trained engravers to produce prints after Old Masters and contemporary painters; he also commissioned work from the painters themselves and, as William Ivins has said, Boydell's patronage 'meant more to many an English painter than did that of His Majesty and a dozen dukes'. He was joined in business by his nephew Josiah, and among their best known undertakings was the *Shakespeare Gallery*,

34 paintings of scenes from the plays, including work by Reynolds, Romney and Benjamin West. Both Boydells became aldermen, John being created lord mayor of London in 1791. For that year the London Directory lists 16 print-sellers (although some authorities consider this an under-estimate) and 110 booksellers, out of a total of some 7,500 London tradesmen. The list includes Robert Sayer, who reissued the Bucks' work in 1774, Carington Bowles, and Molteno, Colnaghi & Co—still surviving as Colnaghi, the well-known Bond Street art dealers.

For the most part, as far as topography is concerned, the Boydells and their fellow publishers concerned themselves with producing illustrations of 'antiquities', picturesque views and the seats of the nobility and gentry. One of the leading publishers of illustrated topography was Alexander Hogg (Plate 4), who issued *England Display'd*, about 1769, *The Complete English Traveller*, 1771 (Plate 5), *The Modern Universal British Traveller*, 1779, Henry Boswell's *Historical Description of New and Elegant Picturesque Views of the Antiquities of England and Wales*, 1785, and G. A. Walpoole's *New British Traveller*, 1790. The engravings in these books can at best be described as undistinguished and many of them were used in more than one volume. John Britton, himself responsible a few years later for several publications of a much higher order, commented that Boswell's *Antiquities* 'has a great number of prints wofully executed both as to drawing and engraving, and copied . . . from any and every source that was accessible.' Hogg was in fact sued for copying from Francis Grose's *Antiquities*, and Boswell was accused of filching the text. Possibly because of the nature of the publications, the names of Hogg's engravers were frequently not given. Grose's volumes were published by S. Hooper, who with C. Sparrow and J. Newton engraved many of the plates. There is certainly a lot of Sparrow's work still around, much more probably than he was ever paid for, but it is of little artistic or technical interest. The addition of allegorical figures, as in 'History Preserving the Monuments of Antiquity' (from Grose, Plate 6), sometimes provides an enlivening touch. Grose's work appeared in instalments between 1773 and 1787, and he made most of the drawings himself.

Thomas Pennant was another antiquarian travelling widely in England, Wales and Scotland during these years. He was accompanied by his servant, Moses Griffith, who had received some training in draughtsmanship and produced the drawings and engravings for his master's published *Tours*, 'far superior in accuracy to those by Francis Grose', said Britton (Plate 7).

The first issue of *The Copper Plate Magazine, or a Monthly Treasure for the Admirers of the Imitative Arts* was published in 1774 by G. Kearsley. It ran for about three and a half years and contained an equal number (42 of each) of

View *of* DERWENTWATER, *a* LAKE, *in* Cumberland.

View *of* BROADWATER, *a* LAKE, *in* Weſtmoreland.

Lodge Sc.

View *of* WINANDER MERE, *another* LAKE, *in* Weſtmoreland.

Plate 4 These Lake District views appeared in one of Alexander Hogg's publications and are printed on peculiarly unpleasant paper. The engravings are by John Lodge

Plate 5 Perspective view of the Castle, or Royal Palace at Windsor, from Alexander Hogg's publication *The Complete English Traveller*, 1771. Like many plates published by Hogg, this one is anonymous. It has little to recommend it, like most—if not all—of the pictorial work issued by this publisher

landscapes, portraits and 'history pieces'. Most of the landscapes were after drawings by the young Paul Sandby and nearly all of them were engraved by Michael 'Angelo' Rooker, son of Sandby's friend Edward Rooker, also an etcher and engraver. Kearsley's *Magazine* began publication the same year that Wedgwood and Bentley's cream-ware service, made to the order of Catherine the Great, Empress of Russia, and 'ornamented with different views of the ruins, country houses, parks, gardens, and picturesque landscapes of Great Britain', was put on exhibition in London before being exported. The catalogue description quoted above gives a good idea of the priorities in scenic depiction at that time. Wedgwood's service and Kearsley's *Magazine* together point to the new importance of topographic representation, and it is interesting to note that it was only the landscapes in the *Magazine* that were reissued a few years later as part of Sandby's *The Virtuosi's Museum*.

Another collection of antiquities that appeared in instalments during this period was the *Antiquities of Great Britain*, containing eighty-four plates, of

Plate 6 This copper engraving by C. Sparrow shows history preserving the monuments of antiquity, in the setting of the side view of Lindisfarne or Holy Island Monastery. It illustrated Grose's *Antiquities* and was published in 1784—six years after Sandby's lively and accurate view of Worcester

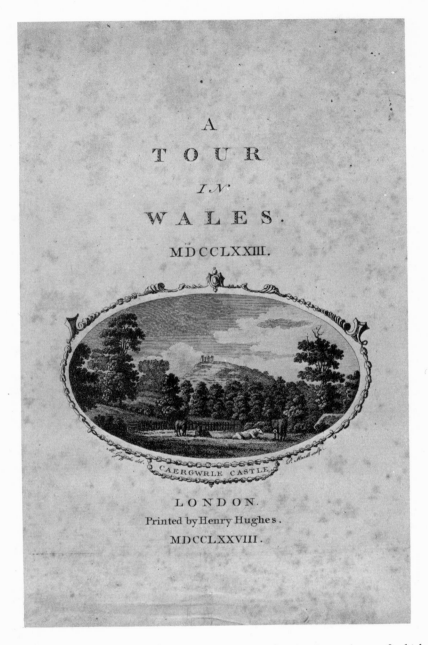

Plate 7 Title-page of Thomas Pennant's *A Tour in Wales*, the first volume of which was published in 1778. The vignette, like the other illustrations in the book, is after a drawing by Pennant's servant, Moses Griffith, and was the work of Peter Mazell, who engraved for many of Pennant's books

which fifty-two were after drawings by Thomas Hearne. Hearne had been apprenticed to Woollett for six years, but eventually he decided to concentrate on drawing and let others execute the plates. His training led him to produce work that provided the engraver with as few difficulties as possible; hence he limited his colour range and gave special attention to trees and skies. His chief engraver was William Byrne who paid Hearne ten guineas for each of his drawings and resold them for eight guineas when he had finished with them. The complete work was bought by the publishers Cadell & David for £1,600 and appeared in two volumes in 1807.

Paul Sandby, whose work spans the whole of the second half of the eighteenth century, was a greater artist than Hearne. Born in 1725, he began his career, as did his elder brother Thomas, as a military draughtsman. In the late 1740s he tried etching on copper, and sold some examples of English and Scottish landscapes through a relative, William Sandby, who was a bookseller. While gaining experience as a watercolour painter he continued practising etching and in 1765 a collection of a hundred of his etchings was sold for £1 7s by Ryland & Bryer, engravers and printsellers of Cornhill, and Jeffrey's Bookshop in St Martin's Lane. In the same year he became a director of the Incorporated Society of Artists but he resigned shortly afterwards with a group of fellow-artists to campaign for royal support for an academy. The Royal Academy came into being in December 1768, with Paul Sandby as a member of its first Hanging Committee. At this time he was the Royal Military Academy's chief drawingmaster, as well as drawing instructor to the sons of George III.

A few years later, Sandby wrote an article entitled 'A Mode of Imitating Drawing on Copper Plates discovered by P. Sandby in the Year 1775'. This mode was the aquatint process, called Aquatinta by Sandby. To be strictly correct, he did not discover it; the process was invented by a Frenchman, Jean Baptiste Le Prince, and Sandby had learned of it through Charles Greville, with whom he had toured on the Continent. But he was one of the first to practise aquatint in England, and he pioneered the use of a spirit ground instead of the dust ground used by Le Prince.

His first publication in this method was *XII Views in Aquatinta* from drawings taken on the spot in South Wales, 1775; this was followed the next year by *XII Views in North Wales*, including the illustration of 'The Iron Forge between Dolgelli and Barmouth', one of the earlier depictions of the industrial age. From 1778 onwards, Sandby issued a series of single folio views, in aquatint, of Worcester (Plate 8), Ludlow, Shrewsbury, Bridgnorth, Eltham and Tonbridge. His military interest was evidenced in four scenes of encampments in

Hyde Park, St James's Park, Museum Gardens and Blackheath. Warwick and Windsor Castles were among his other aquatint subjects. Sandby's earliest work in aquatint may appear a little crude to the modern eye, but his technique quickly improved and his folio views are of very high quality. He was also one of the first artists to venture into Wales at a time when, it has been said, it was 'an unknown land to ordinary Englishmen . . . no one ever thought of travelling in Wales for pleasure only.'

Engravings after Sandby's watercolours appeared in *The Virtuosi's Museum*, which was made up of thirty-six parts each containing three plates and was published complete in 1778. You could subscribe to the whole collection, buy proof impressions of complete sets or take one or more numbers at a time. The engravers were among the leading practitioners of the day and included Cooke, Mazell, Fittler, Walker, Rooker, Chesham, Medland and Angus. The publishers described the undertaking as 'elegant engravings from the designs of one of the first artists in the kingdom at the very moderate price of One Shilling for each plate, instead of the usual demand of from 2s 6d to 5s made for landscapes of an inferior merit. What a cheap and rational amusement then will these Gentlemen possess monthly, for the same consideration that is given for one night's admission to the pit of a theatre!' Many of the same plates appeared in *The Copper Plate Magazine*, published in five volumes between 1792 and 1802, made up of 42 numbered parts; but the fullest collection of engravings after Sandby was the *Select Views in England, Scotland and Ireland*, with 150 plates, published by Boydell in volume form in 1781. Several of Sandby's worn plates were reissued by Palser of Westminster Bridge Road; these were very poor impressions, gaudily coloured by hand. Fifty plates after Paul and Thomas Sandby appeared in Grose's *Antiquarian Repository* and *Antiquities*, and some of Paul's were used in Watts' *Views of Gentlemen's Seats* and in the *Beauties of England & Wales* between 1793 and 1797. As an engraver, Sandby wrote to Morland, he could produce a small plate for five guineas and one 'about the size of a pane of glass' for ten guineas. As with Hearne, Sandby's own knowledge of engraving must have helped him in producing pictures from which others could work without difficulty. His own watercolours, which until his later years concentrated on accurate representations of nature, helped to make that medium fully acceptable to contemporary connoisseurs, comparable, if not equal, to oil painting.

Although overshadowed in reputation by his younger brother, Thomas Sandby was also a fine draughtsman, with a military training, and he became the first professor of architecture of the Royal Academy. For many years he was deputy ranger of Windsor Great Park and he was responsible for designing Virginia Water. In 1754 a set of eight engravings after his drawings of scenes in the park was published, dedicated to the Duke of Cumberland. Paul was one of the engravers, the others being Vivares, Rooker, Austin and Canot; the whole set, reissued by Boydell in 1772, is especially fine in both conception and execution.

Three important collections of views, mainly of country houses, were published in the last two decades of the eighteenth century. William Watts, who had studied with Paul Sandby and Edward Rooker, engraved and published a series of eighty plates with the title *The Seats of the Nobility and Gentry*, between 1779 and 1786. In the following years he produced *Twelve Views of Bath* and *Select Views of London* and some scenes of Turkey and Palestine, but his career as an engraver was terminated when he became blind. It is worth noting that all the best work in English line engraving on copper and steel was done during Watts' lifetime; he was born in 1752 and died in 1851, the year of the Great Exhibition.

Thomas Milton was another landscape engraver with a high reputation in his day. A governor of the Society of Engravers, he was one of the leading members of the profession. He worked on some of the plates after Sandby and on twenty-four Irish views 'from original drawings by the best masters', as well as on some gentlemen's seats and engravings after collections of pictures. William Angus also worked after Sandby, although he concentrated almost exclusively on country houses. He is best known for his collection *The Seats of the Nobility and Gentry in Great Britain and Wales*, a series running from 1787 to 1797. Like Milton's, most of his work is imitative.

Michael Rooker, nicknamed 'Angelo' by Paul Sandby under whom he studied for a time, engraved for both the Sandby brothers and was also a painter of scenery for the Haymarket Theatre. He followed Paul's example in touring the countryside and produced a large number of views, but with less success. His reputation was sufficiently established, however, for him to be commissioned by the Coalbrookdale Company to draw the recently opened Iron Bridge. Engraved by William Ellis, the plate was published in 1782, dedicated to King George III. Centrally placed, the bridge dominates the scene to a degree which visitors to the site must have found somewhat misleading. Francis Klingender commented that 'as a commissioned work, it was no doubt designed to create as favourable an impression as possible, and to gloss over the less attractive elements of industrial Coalbrookdale.'

Industrial Shropshire had attracted the topographers some years before the building of the Iron Bridge. Two engravings by Vivares were published in 1758, after drawings made jointly by Thomas Smith (of Derby) and George Perry. 'The View of the Upper Works at Coalbrook Dale' (Plate 9) shows the top of Abraham Darby's blast furnace, where iron was first smelted with coke as the fuel instead of charcoal. There is plenty of industrial detail in the scene but no attempt to dramatise it has been made; there is no sense of urgency. This was to come later. We are looking, we feel, at a neat, reasonably accurate view, retaining some of the pastoral convention of the earlier part of the century. Clearly work is going on, but at a leisurely pace, and there are as many horses at work as there are men.

Twenty years later, we can see a great change. In 1788 J. and J. Boydell published six engravings of scenes in the Coalbrookdale district after paintings by George Robertson, who died in that year. Robertson had travelled in both Italy and Jamaica, and was a drawing-master and painter of landscape. He was not particularly well known in his time, although he did become vice-president of the Incorporated Society of Artists. He painted six oils of the Ironbridge Gorge, now lost, and it is from these that the engravings were made.

It has been suggested by Francis Klingender that Robertson consciously divided these pictures into two groups, one showing the beauties and the other the horrors of the Dale. In none of them does the bridge dominate the scene as in Rooker's painting. In one painting the bridge features prominently, but it

Plate 9 (*overleaf*) A view of the upper works at Coalbrookdale, engraved by Francis Vivares after a painting by George Perry and Thomas Smith. Published in 1758, it is one of the earliest industrial views and a fine example of copper engraving. The old blast furnace, left centre, belching smoke, was where Abraham Darby I first smelted iron using coke as fuel

is essentially a romantic view with the height of the cliffs of Benthall Edge
greatly exaggerated (Rooker had exaggerated this as well, but to nothing like
the same extent). Sunlight falls on the abutments, and a man with a donkey is
explaining the features to two visitors in the foreground. No one is actually
using the bridge to cross the river. James Fittler engraved the plate and also
another showing the bridge sunlit in the distance, the main emphasis being on
Lincoln Hill, with a row of workers' houses by the riverside and barges being
loaded with coal.

Two plates were engraved by Francis Chesham. One of them, the view from
the bottom of Lincoln Hill, shows the buildings on either side, and the shipping,
in considerable detail; in this view industry seems to be imposing itself on
nature. Chesham's other plate is 'A View of the Mouth of a Coal Pit near
Broseley'. A romantic wood overhangs the pithead, which is depicted with
fascinating detail; the horse-operated gin wheel and the pulleys and ropes used
to raise the coal to ground level, to be taken away in a small wagon running
on rails, can be clearly seen. In the foreground a woman is walking with two
horses with panniers.

Robertson's other two paintings were engraved by Wilson Lowry, himself
a scientist of note and a Fellow of the Royal Society. In one, 'An Iron Work,
for Casting of Cannon; and a Boring Mill, taken from the Madeley side of the
River Severn', industry dominates completely (Plate 10). This is the Calcutts
Ironworks, where eleven cannon could be bored at the same time. In the centre
of the picture are two blast furnaces and there is a damaged watermill on
the right; smoke streams across the sky; there is a clump of trees in the
distance but otherwise nature seems despoiled with only a scrubby bush
here and there surviving. The second of Lowry's plates, 'The Inside of a
Smelting House at Broseley'—possibly an interior view of Calcutts Works—
is of greater interest to the industrial archaeologist. The composition itself is
highly dramatic, the glare of the furnace lighting the right side of the picture,
while a full silver moon can just be seen through an archway on the left.

These engravings after Robertson are of major importance, not only for
what they show but for the way in which they show it. They are both records
of the impact of the new industrial age and interpretations of it in the light of

Plate 10 (*previous pages*) Ironworks, for casting of cannon; and a boring mill, taken from the
Madeley side of the River Severn, Shropshire, engraved by Wilson Lowry after an oil painting
by George Robertson, and published by Boydell 1788. The view shows the Calcutts Ironworks,
with the boring mill to the left of centre. The only building still surviving is the house on the
extreme right

the current ideas of the beautiful, the sublime and the picturesque. Robertson's are not the most spectacular of the Coalbrookdale views; de Loutherbourg's 'Iron Works, Colebrook Dale', aquatinted by W. Pickett and published in *The Romantic and Picturesque Scenery of England and Wales*, 1805, takes priority in this respect, and the same artist's oil painting 'Coalbrookdale by Night' is another superbly powerful example. Well engraved, and with the prestige of the Boydells' publishing house behind it, however, Robertson's series spread the visual impact of the Industrial Revolution far and wide. No other industrial area captured public interest of the time to anything like the extent that Coalbrookdale did. The Barton aqueduct on the Bridgewater Canal and the iron bridge at Sunderland were frequently illustrated but did not attract the more proficient artists or engravers. Some most improbable prints of the aqueduct were produced, leading to the conclusion that although it certainly existed, the engravers had never seen it themselves.

In 1790 John Boydell published his own *Collection of Views in England and Wales*, a folio volume put together from his engravings of his earlier work. Other topographical issues from his firm in Cheapside included eight fine Peak District views after Thomas Smith of Derby. Joseph Farington's *Views in Cities and Towns in England and Wales* appeared in the same year as Boydell's *Collection*. By this time the first of the colour-plate books were appearing and the trade in fine books and prints was doing extremely well. Most of the really handsome—and expensive—volumes were illustrated by coloured aquatints, like the Boydells' *Thames*, with seventy-six plates aquatinted by J. C. Stadler after drawings by Farington (Plate 11), published by W. Bulmer for the Boydells in 1794-6 and reissued many times as it proved so popular. Uncoloured copper engravings continued to be in demand, however, as attested by the popularity of Walker's *Copper Plate Magazine* which, as has been mentioned, contained several engravings after Paul Sandby. The *Magazine* sold for one shilling a number and the engravings, after drawings by Dayes, Varley, Middiman, Orme, Harraden, William Turner, Girtin and J. M. W. Turner, as well as Sandby, were nearly all by John Walker. In 1799 Walker, having retouched the plates, reissued them in one volume as *The Itinerant*; *A Select Collection of Interesting and Picturesque Views in Great Britain and Ireland: Engraved from Original Paintings and Drawings. By Eminent Artists*. Plates from broken up copies of these publications can be easily distinguished: *Magazine* plates have a number and are subscribed as 'Published [date] by Harrison & Co., 18 Paternoster Row, London', while *Itinerant* plates have no numbers and are published by J. Walker, No 16 Rosomon Street. Considerately, they also have 'The Itinerant' printed top left. Some of these plates had remarkable longevity; those by J. M. W.

Plate 11 Thames Head, the first plate in *Views and Scenery on the River Thames*, published by the Boydells 1794–6. All the plates were after Joseph Farington—seventy-six coloured aquatints in all. This example was engraved by J. C. Stadler and shows three gentlemen studying the source of the Thames. Above them can be seen the mast of a boat on the Thames and Severn Canal

Turner and Thomas Girtin were retouched and reprinted, with a preface and biographies, by the printseller Hogarth under the title *Turner's and Girtin's Picturesque Views Sixty Years Hence*. They were issued again by Bentley in 1873 as *Turner's and Girtin's Picturesque Views a Hundred Years Ago*. But by then the poor old things were really past reviving.

The engraved work of J. M. W. Turner needs to be looked at separately in more detail, as does the large amount of work in aquatint which was becoming increasingly popular by the turn of the century. Another major figure in the history of illustrated topography involved with Walker's *Copper Plate Magazine* was John Britton. Born in Wiltshire, he was apprenticed to a London wine merchant, from whose premises he occasionally escaped to visit two nearby booksellers. According to a Biographical Sketch in the *Imperial Magazine*, 1828, these visits benefited him in two ways: 'the perusal of Cheselden's

Plate 12 Monmouth from a neighbouring hill, sepia aquatint from Samuel Ireland's *Picturesque Views on the River Wye*, 1797. This is one of Ireland's more attractive drawings. It was aquatinted by the Dutchman, C. Apostool, who worked for him on other publications

Anatomy, Quincy's *Dispensatory*, Buchan's *Domestic Medicine*, Tissot on Sedentary Diseases, Cornaro on Health and other works of a like kind, had a salutary effect in regulating his mode of living and inducing observation', and also brought him into contact with topographical books of recent years, which he found 'dull and uninviting'. But he met Walker, who persuaded him to produce written accounts of some of the subjects of the *Magazine*. 'The artist's and author's qualifications were quite on a par', wrote Britton later; 'both were very bad and neither would serve to contrast or depreciate the other.'

Then Britton met Samuel Ireland, a print-dealer and engraver, who had published in 1790 *A Picturesque Tour through Holland, Brabant and part of France*, and went on to produce a number of volumes on the Thames, Medway, Avon and Wye. Although Britton did not think much of Ireland's text and embellishments, he liked the 'pretty aquatints' (Plate 12) and thought that he himself could 'with study and patience, produce something equally entitled to public patronage'. He read Burke's essay 'of the Sublime and the Beautiful' and the various writings on the picturesque of William Gilpin, Uvedale Price and Richard Payne Knight, and enjoyed R. Warner's two *Walks through Wales*, 1797 and 1799. Determined to see for himself, he set out on his own walking tour, with maps, compass, two or three books, camera obscura, umbrella and underwear, leaving London on 20 June and visiting Windsor, Oxford, Stratford, Warwick, Birmingham, Church Stretton, Shrewsbury, Welshpool, Ludlow, Ross, Chepstow, Bristol and Bath. The tour took just over three months and Britton meticulously recorded the cost, £11 16s 9d—viewing Blenheim Palace cost him 2s 6d.

Britton's career as a topographer and antiquarian now began in earnest. The first two volumes of his *Beauties of Wiltshire* were published in 1801, with fourteen engravings, mostly from his own drawings, of which, in his own words, 'little can be said in favour'. The publishers, Vernor and Hood, prevailed upon Britton and his friend Edward Wedlake Brayley to undertake a massive topographical study of England and Wales, to appear in monthly numbers, later to be collected into as many volumes as was necessary. In previous years several smaller 'Beauties of England' had been published and proved profitable; Vernor and Hood insisted on retaining this style of title, despite the authors' dislike of it. Eventually the full title of the work was agreed as *The Beauties of England and Wales, or Delineations, Topographical, Historical, and Descriptive, of all the Counties, collected from authentic sources and actual survey*, by E. W. Brayley and J. Britton; 'accompanied with engraved plates of celebrated remains on antiquity, or of architectural elegance, noblemen's and gentlemen's seats, or the grand productions of nature'. It took twenty-five volumes to complete it.

Unlike their publishers, Britton and Brayley were perfectionists. They set out on enormous walking tours to see the country for themselves; by the end of the fifth volume (1804) they had travelled over three and a half thousand miles. By this time the work was selling well, with a circulation of between three and four thousand for each number. There were frequent disagreements with the publishers, however, who were not enthusiastic over the authors' interest in antiquities, preferring to concentrate on the abodes and estates of the landed (and monied) gentry. A few years later both Britton and Brayley withdrew from the project, although Britton came back to contribute Warwickshire and Wiltshire (it is perhaps worth noting that the counties were dealt with in alphabetical order, with no regard for geographical sense). A variety of authors dealt with the counties in the second half of the alphabet, the most notable being James Brewer who added an introductory volume.

The *Beauties* were illustrated by over seven hundred engravings, at least three thousand of each being issued. Many of them can still be found, identifiable by the subscription 'for the Beauties of England and Wales'. Among those who made drawings for the earlier volumes were Benjamin West, George Arnold, Frederick Nash, Edward Dayes, Paul Sandby Munn, John Varley, Thomas Hearne, J. Buckler and J. M. W. Turner; most of the drawings for the later volumes were by J. P. Neale. The engravers, many of whom had been taught the craft by the elder James Basire, included W. Angus, J. Storer, J. Greig, J. Powell, W. Hawkins, J. Roffe, S. Noble, J. Smith, the brothers George and William Cooke, John Pye, J. C. Smith, R. Comte, John Le Keux and S. Rawle. Of this group, Storer and Greig engraved the plates for Brayley's *Antiquarian and Topographical Cabinet*, 1807–11, and the Cookes did much of the work for Turner's *Southern Coast*.

The contemporary interest in topography can be seen from the fact that between 1803 and 1810 Britton himself wrote reviews of nearly one hundred and fifty topographical and antiquarian books for the *Annual Review*. Among his own works were *The Architectural Antiquities of Great Britain* in five volumes, containing about three hundred and fifty plates, and *The Cathedral Antiquities of England*, in fourteen volumes with three hundred and eleven plates. Most of the books he was involved with were illustrated with copper engravings, but an exception was *Picturesque Views of Noblemen's and Gentlemen's Seats*, with aquatints by Richard and William Havell. This, however, was not a financial success. It cost six guineas for twenty plates and a few pages of text, and was discontinued halfway through publication.

Britton's other major undertakings included *Picturesque Views of English Cities* after drawings by George Fennell Robson. This was published in 1826–7, a time of economic depression; Britton tried to get other publishers to take a share in the work but they were not interested. At first he thought of having the drawings reproduced by lithography, but changed his mind out of 'a desire to give occupation to many line engravers whom the circumstances of the times had left without employment.' To maintain the value of the work, only one thousand copies were printed. There was no accompanying text. Robson's *Cities* was followed by *The Picturesque Antiquities of English Cities*, which appeared in six numbers between 1828 and 1830 (Plate 13). This contained sixty engravings, most of them after W. H. Bartlett. John Le Keux engraved most of the plates; J. C. Varrall, Redaway, Woolnoth and Tombleson did the others. There were also a number of woodcuts and ninety-three pages of text. Each number contained ten engravings and four woodcuts, costing twenty-four

Plate 13 Bristol; view of the floating dock, looking south-west. This plate was etched by J. C. Varrall after a drawing by W. H. Bartlett for Britton's *Picturesque Antiquities of English Cities*, published 1830. The churches are distinguished by the number of birds flying by their towers; one for St Stephen (on the left of the picture), two for St Augustine the Less (in the centre) and three for the Cathedral (on the right). Britton dedicated this plate to 'Thomas Garrard, Esq, FSA, Chamberlain of the City of Bristol and a lover of Antiquarian Literature'

shillings for the small paper issue and two guineas for the large. But the work did not prove popular, despite its undoubted quality, and it was expensive by the standards of the time. Britton himself thought it 'the best written and illustrated of all his works', but it did not even cover its production cost. It had appeared, he considered, twenty years too late; the much cheaper steel engravings had taken over and the works of the old school were 'superseded and neglected'. Nevertheless, it is worth noting that Britton did not lose his publishing acumen; among his later works, published 1838-9, was one of the more splendid books of the early railway age, the *Account of the London and Birmingham Railway*, with thirty-seven lithographs by J. C. Bourne. Britton's career was quoted as an example of 'intellectual energy working its way, unprepared by education, and unaided by patronage, from painful obscurity to honourable eminence'. Certainly he was instrumental in improving the standards of topographical writing and illustration, with a continued insistence on high quality in both.

Unlike the Boydells, Britton was not concerned with the export trade in prints. In the closing years of the eighteenth century, we find John Boydell in great trouble. Much of the work he commissioned was intended for export to France; indeed, the text accompanying many of his publications was in both English and French. The Revolution put a sudden stop to this trade; the firm became bankrupt, and much of his stock, including the paintings for the *Shakespeare Gallery*, were sold off by lottery to enable him to clear his debts. Among the better known of the bilingual works was the *Select Views in Great Britain*, engraved by Samuel Middiman and published in parts between 1784 and 1792. This collection was republished as a single volume by Middiman himself in 1814.

The *Select Views* is interesting for more than one reason. It is clearly influenced by the theory of the 'picturesque', and the views chosen show where the artists and publisher thought the picturesque would be most often found. Fourteen scenes are from the Lake District, five from Wales and three each from Derbyshire, Kent and Cornwall. The other places represented are Bath, the Isle of Wight, Lancashire, the Thames, Devonshire, Sussex, Yorkshire, Somerset, the Wye and the Tamar. Exceptionally perhaps, there is only one view of Scotland. Among the artists were Thomas Smith of Derby, William Marlow, Francis Wheatley (best known for his often reproduced 'Cries of London'), Thomas Malton, Samuel Ireland, Lord Duncannon, William Payne (whose contributions are the most pleasing) and Samuel Heironymous Grimm.

Another point of interest is the text, which shows the influence of picturesque theory as markedly as do some of the pictures. As an example, here is the commentary to the view of Keswick Lake.

> The picturesque Scenery surrounding the celebrated Lake of Keswick, possesses a Diversity that must astonish every Admirer of the Romantic. This View, near Lady's Rake, a large opening in the Rocks between Wallow and Barrow Crags, exhibits an Assemblage of the most stupendous Objects near the Lake.
>
> Lowdore Water-Fall, on the Left, is pointed out in this View by a Spray, yet concealed by the Interposition of a Glade of trees skirting the Borders of the Lake.

Beyond, Gowdar-Crag, a formidable Mass, towers over its Base, bulging out in horrid Shapes, pendent and threatening; near the Path, and in the Lake, lie dispersed the huge Fragments of Rocks that have tumbled from its Summit. At the Extremity, Castle-Crag appears of a pyramidal Form; apparently blocking up the Pass to Borrowdale, from whence a grotesque Scene of Rocks opens to the View, of the most singular and opposite Forms, rising in cumbrous Piles, or starting into conical irregular Shapes, with Trees vegetating from their numerous Fissures. Strange Masses are upheld by Fragments, apparently unequal to the Weight they sustain, and appear as if suspended by Magic, forming an awful Precipice from the Base to the Summit; the Changes in their Disposition are infinite, alternately assuming the most fantastic Shapes; and every Step produces a Combination of Objects magnificently great. On the opposite Shore is seen a Range of Mountains . . . those that form the Out Line to the South, lie in fine Order of Perspective, are much broken, and highly picturesque . . .

THE PICTURESQUE AND THE TURNER PRINT INDUSTRY

Picturesque ... picturesque tours ... picturesque views ... the adjective is inescapable. We associate what can be called 'the Picturesque movement' with the late eighteenth century, but William Gilpin was formulating his ideas on the subject in the 1740s while at Queen's College, Oxford. As an artist, Gilpin was inconsiderable; as a thinker, he was sometimes confused and contradictory. But he had a way of asserting his opinions which was easy to understand. Between 1768 and 1776 he toured the country from Kent to the Scottish Highlands, and the accounts of his journeys circulated widely in manuscript many years before they were published. 'Beautiful objects please the eye in their natural state ... Picturesque objects please for some quality capable of being illustrated in painting', he wrote, and it was as a painter that he looked at, and judged, a landscape. Probably because Thomas Rowlandson and William Combe so effectively satirised him in the immensely popular Tours of Dr Syntax, it is Gilpin who is more closely identified with the picturesque movement than some of the greater artists and deeper thinkers.

'Roughness forms the most essential part of the difference between the beautiful and the picturesque', Gilpin wrote in his *Essay on Picturesque Beauty*. This he illustrated by two plates, one showing a scene of smooth, rounded hills and the other a scene with the same substructure but the lines broken with rocks and shrubs and two little banditti figures (who appear in many of his pictures) wandering along a track leading into the centre. Architecture as well as nature came into the same definition. 'A piece of Palladian architecture may be elegant in the last degree ... But if we introduce it in a picture, it immediately becomes a formal object, and ceases to please ... Should we wish to give it picturesque beauty, we must use the mallet, instead of the chisel; we must beat down one half of it, deface the other, and throw the mutilated members around in heaps.' Gilpin also would have liked to use a mallet on Tintern Abbey, where 'a number of gabel-ends hurt the eye with their regularity; and disgust by the vulgarity of their shape.'

Gilpin's own published illustrations were not intended to depict actual scenes but picturesque or general ideas. Looking at an aquatint by Sandby, you always know where you are; but with Gilpin's aquatints it is quite otherwise. Few buildings are more readily recognisable than Ely Cathedral, but you could never identify it from Gilpin's view. For him, as for so many of his contemporaries, the ideal picturesque landscape was to be found in the Lake District (Plate 14). His own tour of the Lakes took place in 1772 and was described in eight manuscript volumes. The printed version appeared in 1786, but by this time the Lakes were widely celebrated, mainly through the popular *Guide to the Lakes* by Thomas West. The first edition of this was published in 1778 and it was reprinted frequently in the following decades. It seems likely that West had imbibed some of Gilpin's ideas; his own work, later editions of which also included Thomas Gray's sensitive account of his 1769 tour, carefully draws the reader's attention to various 'stations' from which the landscape could be viewed to the best advantage. West recommended the use of a Claude glass, as used by Gray, a darkened mirror, slightly convex, in which the tourist, having turned his back upon the scene, could compose the view he wished to enjoy. (Today's tourist is acting in a similar way when he composes his picture on the ground glass screen of a reflex camera.)

At times, Gilpin seems to parody himself. 'Cows are commonly the most picturesque in the months of April and May, when the old hair is coming off,' he wrote. Uvedale Price, author of *An Essay on the Picturesque*, 1794, who supported and developed some of Gilpin's ideas, extended the theory to cover breeds of dogs: 'the Pomeranian, and the rough water-dog, are more picturesque than the smooth spaniel, or the greyhound.' Gypsies and beggars were seen as picturesque objects rather than human beings who might steal from you or demand alms or employment. Factories, foundries and other industrial artefacts were painted with the semblance of ruination and decay.

The picturesque was an offshoot of the larger movement that occupied the eighteenth century—the movement from the classical to the romantic. One of the great engineering triumphs of the century, the canal tunnel at Sapperton taking the Thames and Severn Canal underneath Earl Bathurst's park, with its classical eastern portal at Coates and its castellated Gothic portal at the western end, epitomises this trend. George III and his family visited the tunnel in 1788, shortly before it was opened to traffic, and they were all astonished and full of admiration at what they saw. The tunnel was also evidence of the increase in

Plate 14 Picturesque scene in the Lake District, drawn by William Gilpin. It is one of a series published by Edward Orme in 1810, aquatinted by Dubourg and Humble. No purpose is served by trying to find the exact location of this view—they are all examples of 'the picturesque'

industry and commerce. At this time, however, canals themselves were by no means picturesque; their 'lineal and angular course' with 'sharp parallel edges, naked and unadorned' made them, according to Gilpin, 'disgusting'. Here it is interesting to note that as late as the 1840s Brunel deliberately left a mouth of one of the tunnels near Bath unrepaired after a landslide because it resembled a ruined medieval gateway (Plate 15), and he even trained ivy over it as you can see in J. C. Bourne's *Great Western Railway*.

With the vogue for the picturesque came a great increase in the number of tours and a renewal of interest in the visible remains of the past. These combined to feed the growing appetite for engravings, particularly as illustrations to travel books and guides. In addition to the Tours of West, Gilpin and Gray, and various anonymous volumes, there are Descriptions, Excursions, Tours and Guides by a host of visitors to the Lake District, published in the last thirty

Plate 15 Tunnel number two, near Bristol, from *The Great Western Railway*, J. C. Bourne's superb collection of lithographs showing Brunel's line in operation. The tunnel portal was damaged by a landslide and deliberately left in this 'picturesque' condition

years of the eighteenth century, to be followed by far more in later years when the development of steel engraving reduced the price of books and enabled much larger editions to be printed. The Peak District, Scotland, Wales and the Wye Valley, and the Thames were other areas for adventurous, but not especially dangerous, exploration. The pity is that, on the whole, the books themselves were poorly written. The works of the most perceptive of the travellers, Viscount Torrington and Arthur Young, were not illustrated—although Young did show farmyard implements and model cottages—and the most notable Lake guide, that of Wordsworth, carried plates which the author of the text described as 'intolerable'. He did not want to be associated with them. 'They will please many who in all the arts are most taken with what is worthless', he commented, and the Revd Joseph Wilkinson's 'drawings, or etchings, or whatever they may be called', were omitted when the text of the guide was republished. Wordsworth wrote as a resident, not as a tourist, and as a lover, not merely an admirer, of nature.

Much of the debate on the picturesque stemmed from Edmund Burke's *Philosophical Enquiry into the Origin of our Ideas of the Sublime and Beautiful*, 1757. For Burke, beauty was smooth and gentle and the sublime was terrifying, enormous and obscure. There was a graduated scale of the sublime, in which astonishment comes half-way between respect and terror. This scale was effectively ridiculed by Thomas Love Peacock, that most sensible and forthright commentator on contemporary foibles, in a footnote in *Nightmare Abbey*, 1818, referring to 'Mr Burke's graduated scale of the sublime'. He writes: 'There must be some mistake in this, for the whole honourable band of gentlemen-pensioners has resolved unanimously, that Mr Burke was a very sublime person, particularly after he had prostituted his own soul, and betrayed his country and mankind for £1200 a year: yet he does not appear to have been a very terrible personage, and certainly went off with a very small portion of human respect, though he contrived to excite, in a great degree, the astonishment of all living men.' But this was later. Uvedale Price suggested that the picturesque had its place as an intermediary between the 'sublime' and the 'beautiful', and that it was produced by 'the two opposite qualities of roughness and of sudden variation, joined to that of irregularity'. His neighbour, Richard Payne Knight, replied that objects themselves were not picturesque, but that beauty—or rather 'sensual pleasure'—lay in the eye of the beholder, which, the more it was trained, the more it could perceive. And so the debate went on; but all the while painters such as George Morland were feeding the public taste for this sort of thing (Plate 16).

Morland, it has been said, painted 'from hand to mouth'; he was usually in debt and drank too much. At one time he was painting about a hundred pictures a year, and he painted what would sell easily and cheaply. His rustic studies might almost have been painted according to the recipe of Uvedale Price: 'Among trees, it is not the smooth young beech, nor the fresh and tender ash, but the rugged old oak, or knotty wych elm that are picturesque; nor is it necessary they should be of great bulk; it is sufficient if they are rough, mossy, with a character of age and with sudden variations in their forms.' Price also refers

Plate 16 (overleaf) Uncoloured aquatint by Samuel Alken after a painting by George Morland. The sportsmen are after rabbits. The gnarled oak dominates the scene in typically picturesque style

to the 'wild forester and the worn-out cart-horse . . . old mills, hovels, and other inanimate objects of the same kind'. But it would be surprising if Morland had ever had time to read such deliberations.

One of the grandest series of prints—aquatints in this instance, as in many others—in which picturesque theory is exemplified is *Romantic and Picturesque Scenery of England and Wales*, engraved by W. Pickett after watercolours by Philip de Loutherbourg (Plate 17). The eighteen plates, coloured by J. Clark, were published by Bowyer in 1805, accompanied by a text in English and French. De Loutherbourg's interest in and experience of scene-painting and theatre design—his miniature theatre, the Eidophusikon, was a leading London attraction of the early 1780s—are obvious in his dramatic landscapes. But in the closing years of the eighteenth century, and the early decades of the nineteenth, you cannot escape the adjective 'picturesque' in titles of travel books and sets of illustrations (Plate 18). Captain Fitzchrome, in Peacock's *Crotchet Castle*, 1831, is typical of the amateurs who 'wandered despondingly up and down hill for several days, passing many hours of each in sitting on rocks; making, almost mechanically, sketches of waterfalls, and mountain pools; taking care, nevertheless, to be always before nightfall in a comfortable inn . . .' And in published reproductive illustrations, the picturesque lasted until well into the second half of Victoria's reign; *Picturesque Great Britain* and *The Picturesque Survey of England* were titles of books published in 1874 and 1875 respectively, well after the beginning of photography.

Of course the picturesque fancy had its critics. One was Edward Daniel Clarke, whose *Tour through the South of England, Wales, and Part of Ireland* was made in 1791 and published with eleven aquatints two years later. 'It appears to me,' he wrote, 'that the world is weary of that word *picturesque*, it is forced in upon every occasion; nay, one gentleman, the grand master of landscape, has contrived with the aid of a few muddy sketches, to swell that word to a volume.' Another was Thomas Rowlandson who, as we have mentioned, pictured that same 'gentleman' as the unfortunate Dr Syntax suffering so miserably in pursuit of the picturesque, drenched with Welsh rain and pursued by bulls. Jane Austen, as well as Peacock, made ironic fun of its devotees. And William Daniell avoided the adjective in the title of his *Voyage around Great Britain*.

Nevertheless, picturesque theory—and practice—led to some fine, even superb, work. In his *Observations on the River Wye*, first published 1772, in its

Plate 17 (*previous pages*) Cataract on the Llugwy near Conway, coloured aquatint after Philip de Loutherbourg. This is number 17 of the eighteen plates in his *Picturesque Scenery of England and Wales*, published by R. Bowyer in 1805, with a text in English and French

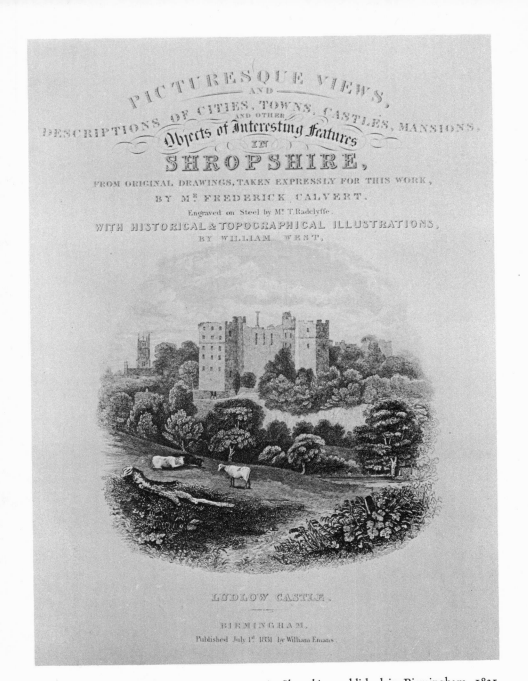

PICTURESQUE VIEWS,
AND
DESCRIPTIONS OF CITIES, TOWNS, CASTLES, MANSIONS,
AND OTHER
Objects of Interesting Features
IN
SHROPSHIRE,

FROM ORIGINAL DRAWINGS, TAKEN EXPRESSLY FOR THIS WORK,

BY MR FREDERICK CALVERT.

Engraved on Steel by Mr T. Radclyffe.

WITH HISTORICAL & TOPOGRAPHICAL ILLUSTRATIONS,

BY WILLIAM WEST,

LUDLOW CASTLE.

BIRMINGHAM.
Published July 1st 1831 by William Emans.

Plate 18 Title-page of *Picturesque Views . . . in Shropshire*, published in Birmingham, 1831.
The drawings are by Frederick Calvert and the steel engravings by T. Radclyffe. Ludlow Castle
is the subject of the vignette

fifth edition in 1800 and translated into several languages, Gilpin wrote that Nature

> works on a vast scale; and no doubt harmoniously, if her schemes could be comprehended. The artist, in the mean time, is confined to a *span*; and lays down his little rules, which he calls the *principles of picturesque beauty*, merely to adapt such diminutive parts of nature's surfaces to his own eye as come within its scope.—Hence, therefore, the painter who adheres strictly to the *composition* of nature, will rarely make a good picture. His picture must contain a *whole*; his archetype is but *a part*. In general, however, he may obtain views of such parts of nature, as with the addition of a few trees or a little alteration in the foreground, (which is a liberty that must always be allowed,) may be adapted to his rules; though he is rarely so fortunate as to find a landscape so completely satisfactory to him. ... The complex scenes of nature are generally those which the artist finds most refractory to his rules of composition.

While it is true that great painters—Gainsborough is an example—were manipulating what they saw in this way before Gilpin wrote these words, we should also remember a collection of engraved work which must rank among the greatest of all, the *Picturesque Views in England and Wales* after J. M. W. Turner. 'He had made several additions to the scenery near the bridge from his own imagination', said Cyrus Redding of one of Turner's sketches for 'Crossing the Brook'. In his watercolours for the *England and Wales*, as in other of his works, Turner did more than make additions to the scenery; he moved cliffs and shorelines, hills and valleys, until he achieved a composition to satisfy the highest standards—his own—of the picturesque.

*　　　　　*　　　　　*

Born in 1775, Joseph Mallord William Turner was the son of a hairdresser, who encouraged the young Turner's early ambition to become a painter by selling his drawings in his shop. In December 1789 he won a place as a pupil at the Royal Academy School, where he learnt perspective and architectural drawing from Thomas Malton. At the age of sixteen he went on the first of many sketching tours around the country, and within a few years the Turner print industry was born. The first engravings after his drawings appeared in *The Copper Plate Magazine* in 1794, views of Rochester and Chepstow engraved by Walker and James Storer; in all, sixteen Turner prints appeared in that publication. For these he received two guineas each. A further sixteen prints were used in three other periodicals—*The Pocket Magazine*, *The Ladies' Pocket*

Magazine, and *The Pocket Print Magazine*—small plates (as might be imagined), not particularly skilfully engraved. These plates reappeared, in poor condition, in *England Delineated*, 1804. All the Oxford Almanacks between 1799 and 1811, with three exceptions, were illustrated by engravings after Turner by the experienced but heavy hand of James Basire, the second of the three generations of that name. Other places sketched by Turner and later engraved included the Isle of Wight, Dunster Castle (the first to be used as book illustrations), Whalley Abbey and other buildings nearby in Yorkshire (for Whitaker's *History of the Parish of Whalley*, 1800–1). One Turner appeared in each of three popular publications: Angus's *Seats of the Nobility and Gentry*, *The Beauties of England and Wales* and the *Essays on Gothic Architecture*. The issues of *Britannia Depicta* between 1803 and 1810 contained seven plates by Byrne after Turner.

So far, the engravings after Turner were in the solid, formal style of the followers of Woollett. But in 1811 John Britton had an engraving made of Turner's painting of Pope's Villa at Twickenham. This was done by the young John Pye, a student of James Heath, engraver to the king. The print appeared in *Fine Arts of the English School* and established Pye's reputation as a master of the art. He was particularly successful with the sky into which he introduced a luminosity rarely attained in reproductive work. Pye was also engaged about this time to engrave Turner's painting of the High Street, Oxford. The plate was first etched by Middiman and the figures in the composition were added by Heath. This large print—23¾ by 16 inches—took two years to complete. It was published singly and was highly esteemed.

At this time, Turner was involved with his *Liber Studiorum*, to some extent modelled on the *Liber Veritatis* of Claude, engraved by Richard Earlom. W. F. Wells, a painter in watercolour and a friend of Turner, is said to have suggested the idea to him and encouraged him to produce a work by which in after years he could be judged. What resulted, however, was a kind of anthology of landscape, which Turner himself divided into various categories: history, pastoral, mountainous, and so on. The plan was to produce 101 plates from drawings made for the purpose, etched on to copper, in most instances by Turner himself, then mezzotinted by one of a team of engravers under Turner's supervision. They were to be issued in numbers, each containing five prints, for fifteen shillings, or twenty-five shillings for proofs. The numbers appeared irregularly between 1807 and 1819, when the project was abandoned because of insufficient interest after 71 prints had been published.

The *Liber* did not begin promisingly. Changing the original plan, Turner engaged F. C. Lewis to etch and engrave the first plate in aquatint for a fee of five guineas. Lewis asked for three guineas more, in view of the labour involved,

Plate 19 Combe Martin, after J. M. W. Turner's watercolour for the *Picturesque Views on the Southern Coast*, completed in 1826. The engraving, on copper, is by W. Miller

but Turner refused and Lewis when he had finished the plate withdrew. The idea of aquatint was dropped and Charles Turner was employed to continue the work in mezzotint, but after completing twenty plates also withdrew because of financial disagreement. The mezzotinters who worked on included William Say, George Clint, S. W. Reynolds (one of the best of the practitioners in this method), Thomas Lupton, J. C. Easling and Henry Dawe. Turner engraved 11 of the plates himself. English landscapes included the junction of the Severn and Wye, Isleworth, Holy Island Cathedral, Morpeth and Dunstanborough; there were also ten Scottish views, of which Ben Arthur and the Fall of the Clyde are good examples.

Although many of the original drawings are full of life and vigour, the end products, printed in brown ink, are generally sombre. Later, the worn plates were reworked by Turner himself and there is not such noticeable deterioration of quality between earlier and later impressions as sometimes occurs. Several of the unpublished plates were engraved in the 1890s by Frank Short. 'The

Stork and Aqueduct' was etched by Turner and engraved by Short, who both etched and engraved the fine drawing of Derwentwater. Short may be judged at least as successful as the early engravers; in the Derwentwater study especially he achieved a superb gradation of tone. But the early engravers suffered, in a way that Short could never have done. For a fee of five guineas Thomas Lupton worked for up to eight weeks on a single plate, with the master instructing, correcting and arguing at every stage.

In 1811 and 1813 Turner toured extensively in the South West making drawings for W. B. Cooke's *Picturesque Views on the Southern Coast of England*, which appeared in sixteen parts between 1814 and 1826 (Plate 19). Each part contained three plates and two vignettes, costing 12s 6d (or eighteen shillings for proof impressions on Imperial quarto). Forty of the plates were after Turner, the others being contributed by Samuel Owen, William Collins, Samuel Prout, Peter de Wint, Luke Clennell and a few more watercolourists. The collected parts were published in volume form in 1826 by a consortium of five London publishers. Most of the engravings were by the Cooke brothers, William and George; four were by William Miller, said to be Turner's favourite engraver, three by Edward Goodall, and the others by W. Radclyffe, J. C. Allen and John Horsburgh. Turner began by asking ten guineas for each drawing, but soon demanded more—twelve and a half guineas and twenty-five India proofs of each plate. It is fair to say that the publisher got his money's worth, with rough seas and plenty of action. Corfe Castle, for example, shows not only the landscape view but women spreading linen out to dry—and look at the great haul of pilchards at St Maws! As for the topography—as Ruskin said, the painter with 'inventive power' does not give the actual facts of his subject but 'the impression it made on his mind'. So while the scenes are recognisable, they are not geographically accurate; cliffs are heightened, the coastline altered, but the essence or sensation of the scene is there. They are, above all, *picturesque* views.

The early impressions of the *Southern Coast* plates are usually good, especially the India paper and the large paper editions. They were reprinted several times: by Nattali of Bond Street, in 1849, under the title *The Antiquarian and Picturesque Tour round the Southern Coast* and by Virtue & Co in the *Art Journal*. The quality of these issues is poor; it is even worse in the 1874 *Turner Gallery*, when the plates were almost worn out. In 1891 they were reworked by J. C. Armytage and republished; these are much more acceptable. Incidentally, the *Southern Coast* provides an interesting comparison of engraving techniques. The same drawing—not by Turner but by Samuel Prout—was engraved for this publication by W. B. Cooke and, earlier, by S. Sparrow for Britton's Devonshire volume in the *Beauties*. Cooke's work is much cleaner and less fussy, while in Sparrow's version a quite unnecessary boat has sailed into the picture.

Other drawings by Turner were engraved by W. B. Cooke for his *Views in Sussex* and *Rivers of Devon*, but after a disagreement their collaboration ceased. The next major English topographical work to be illustrated by him was Whitaker's *History of Richmondshire*, which appeared in parts from 1819 to 1823. Turner made the drawings—twenty of them—in 1817–18, and was paid twenty-five guineas for each. The engravers, who included Middiman, Pye, Varrall, Scott, Archer and Heath, did rather better, receiving between sixty and eighty guineas a plate. The subjects of the drawings for this prestigious publication were selected by a committee of the local gentry. John Buckler, noted for his pictures of buildings, also contributed some illustrations, but they are lifeless compared to Turner's.

The *Richmondshire* was expensive; the large paper issue, of which only 160 were printed of each part, was priced at four guineas a number, and the smaller issue, with a circulation of 550, at two guineas. It cost the publishers, Longman's, nearly £10,000 to produce, but despite its popularity it barely recouped that sum. Outstanding among the plates are Pye's engravings of the junction of the Greta and Tees, and Hardrow Fall, Varrall's Merrick Abbey, Higham's Egglestone Abbey and Rawle's Brignall Church. Ruskin thought that Turner's Yorkshire drawings had 'the most heart in them, the most affectionate, simple, unwearied, serious finishings of truth'. Again, there were several reprints; by Nichols & Son in 1843, and in the *Art Journal* and the *Turner Gallery*. And again the quality was poor; as with the *Southern Coast*, only Armytage's reworking of the plates in 1891 produced anything worthwhile.

The team of engravers were in action again for *The Provincial Antiquities of Scotland*, with text by Sir Walter Scott, published between 1819 and 1826. Turner provided half of the twenty-two illustrations, the rest being contributed by John Thomson of Duddingston. As the established artist, Turner was paid twice as much as Thomson, but he did not go out of his way to help his Scottish collaborator. Scott and Turner did not get on together; Scott described him as a man who would 'do nothing without cash and anything for it'.

Work on Turner's final copper-engraved venture, *Picturesque Views in England and Wales*, began in 1826. This, described as his 'central and most ambitious work in black and white', was originally devised by the engraver Charles Heath, together with a firm of printsellers, Jennings & Co; there were to be 120 engravings of towns, landscapes and ancient buildings, but in the event only ninety-six were published. As with previous publications they were issued in numbers, beginning in 1827. The first collected volume, with sixty plates, came out in 1832; the royal quarto version cost ten guineas and at the top of the list of alternatives came the volume of India proofs, with the etchings, Colombier folio for forty-eight pounds. The second volume contained only thirty-six plates, but later the plates were redivided to make two volumes of equal size. For each drawing—some of which were made specially while others were based on earlier sketches—Turner received between sixty and seventy guineas, while the engravers were paid from eighty to one hundred pounds for each plate. Most of the engravers had worked for Turner before, but there were a few new recruits. As usual, Turner supervised them closely. Writing about three decades later, C. W. Radclyffe, an artist who had worked with some of these men, commented as follows:

> The engraver has not only to work for but with the painter. Turner understood this, for there were few, if any, of the plates engraved from his works upon which there are not traces of his own hand—changes in colour, and form, and effect: happy suggestions—a bit of dark, a point of light, a new sweep of line, an alteration of mass of light and shade—worked out in consultation with the engraver and by him translated from rough hints into effective and intelligible shape.

Radclyffe went into some detail on the problems faced by the engravers, which those who have seen the original watercolours will readily appreciate.

> Take a picture or drawing by Turner in his latter time, full of mystery, and apparently with no accurate drawing in it. First, a reduction has to be made to a scale. The original may be full of the most delicate architectural work, crowded, perhaps, with figures—all, at first glance, a shapeless mass, but all requiring, for the engraver's purpose, to be put into order, and to be submitted to Turner's critical eye. When the plate gets well into progress, then comes the question of colour—a bit of bright orange, or scarlet, or blue; how shall it be rendered in black, or white, or gray? Turner knows; but the engraver dare not ask him until the plate is in such a condition as to require touching. I have seen engravers perfectly bewildered as to what they should do in such cases. All who have studied Turner's work will feel the immense difficulty in translating them into black and white . . .

Yet the engravers managed, sometimes supremely well. Look, for example, at Miller's Carew Castle and Durham, Wallis's Bolton Abbey and Dudley (Plate 20), Higham's Ely Cathedral, Willmore's Richmond from the moors (a

touch of humour here, the dog the little girl is playing with in the foreground is wearing her hat), and his superbly atmospheric renderings of Ullswater and Winander-mere (Windermere). It has been well observed that in the *Views* every hour of the day is represented and every phase of the weather and season. They mark the very summit of achievement in line engraving.

Nevertheless, for Charles Heath the *Picturesque Views* proved a financial disaster. When the project ended in 1838, the plates and the engravings that had not been sold were auctioned. Turner himself, by this time moderately wealthy, bought them for three thousand pounds and would accept no offer to republish them. They were still among his effects at his death in 1851, having escaped the fate that had befallen the plates from the *Southern Coast* and *History of Richmondshire*.

In his invaluable study, *The Engraved Works of Turner*, W. S. Rawlinson records that engravings were made from over eight hundred of the painter's works. The first line engravings on steel appeared in the late 1820s, mostly small plates for annuals such as *The Keepsake* and *The Literary Souvenir*. Leaving aside his studies of continental scenery, Turner's finest steel-engraved work is probably the illustrations for the poems of Scott and Samuel Rogers. Perhaps neither of these would rank among the foremost poets of their day but both were wealthy and influential and assured of wide sales. Henry Le Keux, J. B. Allen, W. R. Smith, Wallis, Willmore, Miller and the two Cousen brothers were among Turner's steel engravers.

The engravings for Rogers' *Poems* (Plate 21) were issued separately from the text as proofs, with the Colombier proofs before lettering costing four guineas. The engravers received between thirty and forty guineas for each plate, mostly vignettes averaging three and a half by two and a half inches. Originally Turner was to be paid fifty pounds a drawing, but as this would have proved too expensive for the publishers he agreed to loan the drawings for five pounds each. Thomas Stothard also contributed illustrations to Rogers' best known poem, 'Pleasures of Memory', and these were engraved by Bewick's sometime pupil Luke Clennell. These are solid, rectangular statements, good enough of their kind but having nothing of the atmospheric quality of the plates after Turner which seem somehow to materialise out of the page, always exquisitely right. Ruskin described Turner's vignettes for Rogers' *Poems* as 'the loveliest engravings ever produced by the pure line' (Plate 22). Prior to these line engravings, a series of mezzotints on steel from Turner's paintings had been

Plate 20 (previous pages) J. M. W. Turner's view of Dudley, one of the few industrial scenes he portrayed, engraved for *The Picturesque Views of England and Wales* by R. Wallis

WRITTEN IN

THE HIGHLANDS OF SCOTLAND,

SEPTEMBER 2, 1812.

BLUE was the loch, the clouds were gone,
Ben-Lomond in his glory shone,
When, Luss, I left thee; when the breeze
Bore me from thy silver sands,

Plate 21   A page from Samuel Rogers' *Poems*, 1830. Turner's vignette of Loch Lomond has been superbly engraved on steel by Miller

Had won his soul; and rapturous Fancy shed
Her golden lights, and tints of rosy red.
But ah! few days had passed, ere the bright vision fled!
　　When Evening tinged the lake's ethereal blue,
And her deep shades irregularly threw;
Their shifting sail dropt gently from the cove,
Down by St. Herbert's consecrated grove;
Whence erst the chanted hymn, the tapered rite
Amused the fisher's solitary night:

Plate 22 St Herbert's Chapel, another illustration to Rogers' *Poems* after J. M. W. Turner.
Henry Le Keux was the engraver of this beautiful vignette

published by W. B. Cooke. This series, one of the very first in which steel was used, was the *Rivers of England*, sometimes known as *River Scenery*, comprising eighteen plates after Turner and two after Girtin, published between 1823 and 1827. It was intended to follow the *Southern Coast* and indicates that, for a time at least, Turner had made his peace with Cooke after their earlier disagreement. There was difficulty with the metal at first, three of the plates breaking and having to be remade. The mezzotinters included Thomas Lupton, William Say and S. W. Reynolds, all of whom had worked on the *Liber*, and Charles Turner, J. Bromley and G. H. Phillips. Some of the drawings were made on Turner's journey to Scotland in 1822, but obviously not all of them, unless he travelled by a particularly circuitous route. The rivers depicted are the Tyne, Tweed, Aire, Coquet, and the junction of Eamont and Lowther, all of which he might have sketched on such a trip, but not the Colne, Medway, Dart, Okemont and Arun, which are included as well. P. G. Hamerton made the rather silly criticism that Turner had chosen unfamiliar rivers, instead of the mighty Thames and Severn, but Turner was less concerned with the river itself than with the scenery around it. In most cases he uses a low viewpoint to emphasise the hills around, topped often by the seemingly inevitable castle. 'Kirkstall Lock on the River Aire' is one of the few in which the river has some prominence. Generally the plates are fine if, as almost always with landscape mezzotint, a little dark, but many poor quality reissued examples are in circulation, often recently and inappropriately hand-coloured. Most critics consider the later series, *Rivers of France*, to be superior in quality. Towards the end of their production, another series, *The Ports of England*, was begun but it was abandoned after only six plates, all by Lupton, had appeared between 1826 and 1828.

Throughout his career, Turner's work for the engravers was a source of conflict. There were frequent arguments over money. Thomas Lupton was paid five guineas for a mezzotint, and he itemised what it cost him as follows:

Copper plate, 7s 6d: mezzotint ground 15s. My own labour seven or eight weeks. As to provings innumerable, resulting from the difficulty of obtaining an agreeable colour as nearly approaching to that of the drawings as possible; consequently the proving was not only difficult but expensive, even to the amount of two or three shillings a time. N.B. I forgot the beginning. The engraver had also to lay the etching ground and trace the subject on the plate for the painter to etch, which was his uniform practice.

F. C. Lewis, to whom Turner had refused to pay more than five guineas, received a minimum of fifteen guineas for each of the Claude drawings he engraved.

Conflict of a different kind occurred over Turner's efforts to have his coloured vision translated into the black and white of an engraving. So much work was done on the plates that they quickly wore out; it was possible to obtain only about thirty really good impressions from one of the *Liber* plates. And there was also what might be called a critical conflict, for Turner has been accused of playing down to public taste for the sake of increasing the sales of the engravings. In this connection it is worth recalling John Pye's story of Turner a few years before his death. Turner was walking beside the Tweed with a friend when Norham Castle came in sight. Turner bowed to it, saying 'It was my drawing of Norham Castle that brought me into public notice.' This was a drawing made in 1798, but the castle was drawn many times afterwards and engraved for the *Liber* and *Rivers of England* by Heath and by Miller.

Turner died in 1851, having virtually given up working with his engravers for the last fifteen years of his life. But what has been described as 'the Turner Print Industry' continued to flourish. Some of its later products were worthy of those produced under his own supervision, such as the 'Harbours of England', a republication by Ruskin of the *Ports of England*, with seven additional plates. Less satisfactory, however, were the plates of the *Turner Gallery*, 1859, sixty in all, most of them engraved by men who had worked for him during his lifetime, including Miller, Willmore, Brandard and Goodall. 'They show an even greater brilliance in their cutting', wrote Arthur M. Hind, 'but all the subtler gradations of light, which Turner gained by repeated correction on the proofs, are wanting.'

3

AQUATINT AND LITHOGRAPHY

The first English prints in aquatint were made by Peter Burdett in or about 1771 after paintings by John Mortimer and Joseph Wright. Paul Sandby, however, was the first Englishman to use it extensively, in his Welsh landscape views after his own originals, published in 1775 and 1776. It remained a moderately popular printing process for about sixty years and was the medium for some of the very finest topographical work, much of it hand-coloured. The earlier aquatints were uncoloured or, like Sandby's *Views in South Wales*, printed in sepia ink. William Gilpin's *Observations on the River Wye*, first published 1782, was illustrated by tinted aquatints, as were most of his other volumes, while Hassell's *Tour of the Isle of Wight*, 1790, was embellished with thirty aquatints tinted yellow, blue, pink or brown. In later years, many collections were issued in both uncoloured and coloured versions and priced accordingly.

The earliest sets of English topographical coloured aquatints appeared in 1791; they are Tomkins' *Eight Views of Reading Abbey*, J. Fittler and J. Love's *Views of Weymouth* and six plates of *Castles in England and Wales*, etched by J. Schnebbelie and aquatinted by G. J. Parkyns after drawings by James Moore. The colouring—added by hand to each individual print—greatly increased the cost; the full set of Moore's *Castles* appeared in 1792, consisting of seventy-two uncoloured plates as the coloured version had proved too expensive a proposition. Within a few years the great productions of the major publishers, the Boydells, Ackermann and Bulmer, began to appear, although the market, hindered by the difficult economic conditions of the 1790s, took some time to develop. It was not until 1805 that the number of colour-plate books published in a single year reached double figures. In 1815, twenty books appeared; between 1819 and 1825 the total published was 166. After 1825, the figures rapidly declined, although many of the titles were reissued several times in the first half of the century.

The Boydells' major colour publication was the *History of the River Thames*, containing seventy-six plates aquatinted by J. C. Stadler after the watercolours of Joseph Farington. The two volumes, originally published 1794–6, were intended to be a major instalment of a series on the 'Principal Rivers of Great Britain', which never materialised. Farington was a better diarist, perhaps, than a painter; the plates are attractive but generally lifeless. They have less appeal than the two other important collections of coloured Thames scenes: *Picturesque Views of the Thames*, 1812, by the Havell family, aquatinted by the brothers Robert and Daniel from the drawings of William, and the superb *Picturesque Tour of the Thames*, aquatinted by R. G. Reeve from drawings by William Westall and Samuel Owen.

The Havells' *Views* consisted of 12 plates, finely detailed and beautifully coloured. These are also of interest because they show the river at work; in some of them one can see the big 'west country' barges, either being towed from the bank or manoeuvred in mid-stream. In one plate the Datchet Ferry is being winched across the river with a horse and cart on board; another shows the City Stone in rural surroundings at Staines. William Havell was a leading watercolourist and Robert and Daniel translated his originals so expertly that good impressions could almost pass for watercolours themselves.

The Westall and Owen *Tour* contained twenty-four plates, nineteen by Westall and five by Owen. Reeve aquatinted fifteen of them; the others were by C. Bentley, J. Baily and J. Fielding. William Westall, the younger brother of Richard, a popular oil painter of the period, was employed as a land-scape draughtsman to an expedition to Australia at the age of twenty and spent five years overseas visiting Australia, China and Bombay, and survived a shipwreck in the course of his travels. On his return to England he worked for the publishers Ackermann and Rodwell Martin and was sufficiently skilled to make both aquatints and lithographs from his own drawings. Among his aquatints were views of Yorkshire caves, 1818, *Abbeys and Castles in Yorkshire* and *Views in the Lakes*, both 1820, and *Fountains Abbey and Studley Royal*, 1846. He also supplied originals for a number of steel-engraved views. His Thames plates are all of high quality; yet they are surpassed in brilliance and interest by those after Samuel Owen. Owen's pictures are of the tidal reaches; he was a marine painter and his interest in this part of the river allowed him to develop to the best advantage. His illustration of Tilbury Fort, showing a variety of shipping including the steamship *Venus*, and his view of the Custom House and shipping in the Upper Pool, must rank among the very highest achievements in aquatinted scenes. Westall illustrated the quieter reaches of the river, although there are no views above Oxford, apart from a vignette by Owen on the title-page. His plates are certainly comparable with Havell's, and the whole book is one of the most splendid and desirable ever produced—probably the finest on the much-illustrated Thames.

Many of the most important collections of aquatints were published by Rudolph Ackermann, who opened his print shop in the Strand in 1795, after emigrating from Germany and marrying an Englishwoman. His shop—the Repository of Arts—eventually replaced the Boydells' establishment as the focal point of the print trade. Aquatint became his speciality, and he employed a large number of colourists, many of them emigrés, to finish the plates, most of which were printed in only one or two basic colours. He also attracted major artists, of whom probably the best known are Thomas Rowlandson and the elder Pugin. Pugin did the buildings and Rowlandson the figures for some of Ackermann's most successful undertakings, including the three volumes of *The Microcosm of London*, collected in 1810 from a succession of monthly parts. Of the 154 plates, fifty-four were aquatinted by J. Bluck and twenty-nine by Farington's engraver, Stadler. Bluck and Stadler also worked on the majority of the plates for the well-known Oxford and Cambridge views, again first issued in monthly parts and published in volume form in 1814 and 1815 (Plate 23). These were the work of Rowlandson, Pugin and Westall. The volumes themselves were expensive for their time, costing between sixteen and twenty-seven pounds according to page size. Other major Ackermann publications included the *Public Schools and Colleges*, with forty-five aquatints and four line engravings by Bluck, Stadler, D. Havell and Bennett after drawings by Westall, Pugin, McKenzie and John Gendall—who collaborated with Westall and T. H. Shepherd in the *Views of Country Seats* which appeared between 1823 and 1828—and the *Picturesque Tour of the English Lakes*, with forty-eight coloured aquatints all engraved by T. H. Fielding, thirty-five of them after his own drawings and twelve after drawings by J. Walton—the remaining one was by Westall. The colouring of these plates, however, was less subtle and they do not have the same appeal as the Oxford and Cambridge aquatints. There was also a noticeable difference in the original price, a complete set of the *Lakes* costing £3 13s 6d, or six guineas on large paper.

Plate 23 (overleaf) Cambridge from the Ely Road, coloured aquatint by J. C. Stadler after William Westall, from Ackermann's *Cambridge*. The plate was first published in 1806; this particular print is watermarked 'J. Whatman, 1812'. It is a good example of Westall's detached, undramatic style; the colouring is especially delicate

One of the rarest of Ackermann's coloured books, first published in 1831, three years before the death of the founder of the firm, was *Coloured Views on the Liverpool and Manchester Railway*, with sixteen plates engraved by H. Pyall and S. G. Hughes after drawings by Thomas Talbot Bury. Bury was a pupil of the elder Pugin and worked with his son under the general direction of Barry on the Houses of Parliament. These plates, of the greatest interest to railway historians, were reprinted in 1977. One of them, 'The Tunnel', is particularly interesting because in its first state it showed a locomotive actually steaming through the tunnel, contrary to the Liverpool and Manchester Railway Act which stipulated that this was forbidden. The second state showed the locomotive without its chimney, but with the smoke still discernible. For future issues the plate had to be reworked, the locomotive being removed entirely and the wagons shown attached to a hauling cable as the Act required. Bury also drew *Six Coloured Views of the London and Birmingham Railway*, engraved by J. Harris, C. Hunt and N. Fielding, published for the price of twelve shillings in 1837.

Among Ackermann's numerous publications should be mentioned *Westminster Abbey*, by Pugin and McKenzie, and—at the other end of the scale perhaps—the very many plates for the *Repository of Fine Arts* magazine. He also published the key work on lithography, Senefelder's *Complete Course of Lithography*, 1819, and gave great encouragement to the practitioners of this method—many of the *Repository* plates were lithographs. To many print enthusiasts he is best known as the publisher of Rowlandson's illustrations to William Combe's three Dr Syntax books, whose popularity has endured despite the frequent issue of inferior reprints.

A prolific artist whose work was reproduced in aquatint was John Hassell, born 1767, a friend and biographer of George Morland. He produced two extraordinary books, *The Art of Drawing in Water Colours* and *Aqua Tinta*, which were published in monthly parts and consisted of reproductions of drawings by some of the better known watercolourists of the time, including William Payne, David Cox, John Varley and Thomas Girtin, depicted in four stages—the etched outline, single colour aquatint, yellow washed aquatint and fully coloured. His own work, much of which he aquatinted and published himself, is quaintly attractive but not particularly striking (Plate 24). An early production was the *Tour of the Isle of Wight*, one of the first of the guides to that oft-described resort. This was followed by the *Picturesque Guide to Bath and Bristol Hotwells*, 1793, in which Julius Caesar Ibbetson and John Laporte collaborated with him, and some years later by the first of the twenty-four parts of his *Picturesque Rides and Walks . . . round the British Metropolis*. This comprised 120 views and was collected into two volumes in 1818. While on one of these rides, or walks, he came across the Grand Junction Canal and later revisited it, finding the navigation 'directing its course through scenes of undiminished beauty, and replete with delightful prospects, uniformly pictures-que, and sometimes grand'—very different from Gilpin's response some decades earlier. His *Tour of the Grand Junction*, with twenty-four pretty but rather odd little plates (he could not draw a lock), appeared in 1819. Other publications by Hassell were *Pleasure and Sport on the Thames* and (yet another) *Noblemen's and Gentlemen's Seats*, both dated 1823.

One of the most impressive figures in the history of aquatinted topography is William Daniell, born two years after Hassell. In 1784 Daniell's uncle, Thomas, took him to India where they spent many years touring, painting and sketching. Their *Oriental Scenery*, in six volumes, five of which were aquatinted by William, appeared in 1808. Four years earlier he had produced six superb views of London, a blend of placidity and grandeur, of which the outstanding plates are London Bridge and Somerset House. He also brought out a set of eight aquatints of the London docks between 1800 and 1813.

In 1814 Daniell, in company with Richard Ayton, began on his *Voyage around Great Britain*, which was to take eleven years to complete. Starting at Land's End, they travelled up the northern coast of Cornwall and Devon (Plate 25) and worked their way along the coastline of Wales and Anglesey, north-west England, the whole of Scotland including many of the islands, down the eastern seaboard and along the south coast back to Land's End. At least, Daniell did; Ayton accompanied him as far as Scotland but was unable to complete the whole journey and died at the age of thirty-seven. Daniell then took over the writing of the text, but his is poor stuff compared with Ayton's lively and informative prose.

The *Voyage* was a remarkable achievement. Daniell toured during the summers, returning to London to engrave the drawings he had made on the spot. They were printed in brown and grey-blue and the rest of the colouring was added by hand by a team employed by William Timms of Hampstead Road. The quality of the colouring is exceptional; delicate and restrained, it compares favourably with even the best of Ackermann's productions. 'Daniell excels in suggesting the warm haze that hangs over a summer sea, or sunlight

Plate 24 (*overleaf*) Aust, Old Passage-House near Thornbury, Gloucestershire, coloured aquatint by and after John Hassell. Aust is on the Severn, and a ferry plied between Aust and Beachley, on the Welsh bank, until replaced by the road bridge in 1964. This is a large plate for Hassell, who usually worked on a much smaller scale

Plate 25 Lynmouth, on the coast of North Devon, drawn and engraved by William Daniell and first published 1814. This is one of the earlier plates, all coloured aquatints, from Daniell's *Voyage around Great Britain*

playing on the roofs of a fishing village, or rugged cliffs where sea-gulls swoop in circling flight', wrote Martin Hardie. He was attracted by lighthouses, by boats drawn up on the sand, by the activity of shipping and by the shapes of quays and harbours. In conditions of discomfort and possibly even danger he depicted the rugged glories of the Scottish coastline; some of his illustrations of the Inner Hebrides he extracted and sold separately on account of their geological interest. Several plates show activity as well as scenery—men at work in the black marble quarry near Red Wharf Bay in Anglesey, for example —and a view of the Clyde estuary includes the first pictorial representation of a steamboat. Pictures of bustling seaports like Liverpool and Sunderland give evidence of contemporary commerce and industry, while some of today's busy coastal resorts, like Southend and Margate, are shown as they were at the very beginning of the tourist age.

The *Voyage* was collected into four volumes and at sixty pounds was comparatively expensive. The plates were reissued later in the century but with inferior colouring and some alterations in the attire of the figures to keep up with contemporary fashion in dress. Issues on a heavy card-type paper are of early date, but those on paper with a shiny finish are later. The plates are still in existence, and the Tate Gallery has recently reprinted six of them in an uncoloured state. It is worth noting that Daniell's *Voyage* was one of the few major projects that was actually brought to completion and, apart from Ayton's contribution, it was very much a single-handed effort (Plate 26). Daniell seems to have enjoyed his travels on the whole; Farington, whom he visited on his return from the Western Isles in 1815 to show him his sketches, noted that 'he was much gratified with the Hospitality he found everywhere, but noticed the general deficiency in order and cleanliness and of the coarse appearance of the female attendants.' But the weather was mostly fine, which must have been some compensation.

The topographical work in aquatint described so far was all finished by hand-colouring, and was therefore costly. Among the less expensive produtions were Samuel Ireland's topographical books, illustrated with sepia aquatints in what might be described as the 'penny plain' version. A river specialist, his *Picturesque Views on the Thames*, with fifty-two plates, was published in 1792, and was followed by volumes on the Medway, the Wye and the Avon. Ireland's drawings were aquatinted by a Dutchman, C. Apostool; it would not be unfair to say that neither was an artist of the first rank. The Wye tour volume in particular was criticised by an energetic clergyman, the Revd G. J. Freeman, in his *Sketches in Wales*, a diary of three walking excursions between 1823 and 1825. Freeman called the aquatints 'wretched' (his own book was

Plate 26 Tobermory, on the Isle of Mull, another coloured aquatint from the *Voyage around Great Britain* by William Daniell. These plates are unsurpassed for their subtle gradations of tone and their confident composition. This example, one of the large number of Scottish views, was first published in 1818

illustrated by lithographs by T. M. Baynes) and he mocked Ireland's account of a waterfall several hundred yards long followed by an 'immense cataract' on the course of the infant Wye down Plynlimmon. 'In the Andes he could not have employed greater diction', he added. But these same plates were described by John Britton as 'pretty'; they certainly provide a useful record of the bridges and river craft, and some of them are quite attractive. Samuel Ireland's son was the notorious forger of Shakespearean manuscripts, including two supposed plays, which deceived some contemporary scholars for a time, and there was suspicion that Samuel himself was involved. Ireland also made the drawings for *Picturesque Views of the Severn*; these were lithographed by F. Calvert and published with a text by Thomas Harral in 1824, many years after Ireland's death.

Sepia-printed aquatints were also produced by Frederic Christian Lewis, a finer and far more sensitive artist than Ireland but similarly attracted to river scenery. He studied engraving under Stadler; later in life he engraved about a hundred plates after Claude and several after the great Italian masters, including Raphael and Michelangelo. He aquatinted some of Girtin's *Views of Paris* and was considered one of the leading aquatint engravers of his time. Turner employed him on the first of the plates for the *Liber*, but, as we have seen, disagreement over fees led to Lewis's withdrawal from the project. Lewis himself was a landscape painter, exhibiting at the Water Colour Society and the Royal Academy. He was also a publisher, and his three collections of views, *Picturesque Scenery of the River Dart* (Plate 27), 1821, *Scenery of the Tamar and Tavy*, 1823, and *Scenery of the River Exe*, 1827, were etched and published by himself, mostly from his own paintings and drawings. He used sepia aquatint for the Dart engravings (Plate 28), which he described as 'executed to form as nearly as possible facsimiles of the drawings and therefore calculated to interest not only the admirers of Nature and those unacquainted with the Country, but also to form a set of studies for the learners of Landscape Drawing.' The Dart illustrations in general are carefully composed and show subtle gradation of tone (Plate 29). There are thirty-five plates altogether, all but seven after Lewis's own originals.

In 1843, Lewis brought out his final collection, *Scenery on the Devonshire Rivers*, with twenty-five plates, some etchings and some mixed method—a combination of etching, aquatint and mezzotint—many of them new versions of paintings reproduced by other methods in earlier publications. The didactic tone noted in the Dart volume is apparent here in the Introduction where Lewis, writing in the third person, says that 'having to the best of his ability brought upon his transcripts from Nature the principles of Art, he thought that a few Engravings from the Pictures would teach something to those lovers of Nature, who are less experienced in Art than himself, and be favourably received by and afford pleasure to the more cultivated, for the truths both of Art and Nature which the Author believes they contain'. After this example of his prose, we can perhaps be grateful that he published his plates without a written commentary. The plates are accomplished and attractive: 'Mill at Peter Tavy' (Plate 30), 'Hill Bridge' (Plate 31) on the Tavy, and 'Mill near Bridestow', on the River Okement, are three very good examples and the volume as a whole is a splendid collection.

As with the Havells, engraving and painting was a family occupation. Frederic's brother George Robert Lewis made both the drawings and engravings for the *Bibliographical and Picturesque Tour* of Dr Frognall Dibdin, a journey through France and Germany; another brother, William, exhibited at the Royal Academy. Of Frederic's sons, John was trained as an engraver and etcher; he later became very popular as a watercolour painter and was president of the Society of Painters in Water-Colours in 1857, the year after his father died. Another son, F. C. Lewis, painted many Indian scenes which were

Plate 27 Scene below Holne Cottage, plate 11 from Frederic Christian Lewis' *Scenery of the River Dart*. The first plate is the etching and the second the sepia aquatint, all the work being done by Lewis himself. The plates are dated 1820 and the collection was published in 1821

Plate 28 (*overleaf*) Holne Bridge, plate 21 from F. C. Lewis' *Scenery of the River Dart*, sepia aquatint, 1820

Plate 30   Mill at Peter Tavy, drawn, etched and engraved by Frederic Christian Lewis. This is
plate 6 of one of Lewis's later publications, *Scenery of the Devonshire Rivers*, 1843. It is a 'mixed
method' plate, with etching, aquatint and mezzotint combined

engraved by a third son, Charles. In all, the Lewis family made a major contribution to the artistic achievement of the nineteenth century.

It is worth mentioning one more work, briefly referred to in the Introduction,
in which sepia aquatint was used. This is the *Travels of Cosmo the Third, Grand
Duke of Tuscany, through England during the Reign of King Charles II*. These
travels took place in 1669, but the translation (the text was in Italian) did not
appear until 1821, when it was published by J. Mawman and illustrated by
thirty-nine sepia aquatint plates, showing 'the Metropolis, Cities, Towns and
Noblemen's and Gentlemen's Seats as delineated at that period by artists in the
suite of Cosmo' (Plate 32). The plates have a solid, formal simplicity about them.

Plate 29   (*previous pages*) Spitchwick Lodge from Holne Chase, plate 16 of F. C. Lewis's
Scenery of the River Dart, sepia aquatint, 1820

Plate 31 Hill Bridge, on the River Tavy; plate 20 of F. C. Lewis's *Scenery of the Devonshire Rivers*, 1843

Cosmo pottered about England quite amiably; he was a young man when he undertook this tour, but his death in 1723 terminated 'a reign the most unjust and dissentious that Tuscany had ever known'.

Aquatint was popular in its day but never achieved the prestige of mezzotint. Arthur Hayden devoted only eight pages to aquatint in his study of old prints first published in 1906. He mentioned the work of Thomas Malton, and Stadler's plates for *The Picturesque Scenery of Great Britain*, after de Loutherbourg, but there is only a passing reference to one of the Havells and merely a

Plate 32 (*overleaf*) Newmarket, one of the 39 sepia aquatint plates illustrating the *Travels of Cosmo the Third, Grand Duke of Tuscany, through England, during the Reign of King Charles II* (1669). The text was translated into English and published by J. Mawman in 1821. The aquatints from the original drawings by an Italian artist in Cosmo's entourage were engraved by T. H. Shepherd

few words about the Daniells. He gave most space to some oval aquatints by John Hill after drawings by Charles Dibdin—author of a number of sailors' songs—pleasant, picturesque views illustrating Dibdin's heavily titled *Observations on a Tour Through Almost the Whole of England And A Considerable Part of Scotland*, which consisted of a series of letters 'Addressed to a Large Number of Intelligent and Respectable Friends'. Hayden did say that 'aquatint was too little regarded by leading authorities on print collecting'; a comment borne out also by the fact that Arthur M. Hind, certainly a leading authority, gave it a mere five pages out of the 340 in his *History of Engraving and Etching*. In recent years, with the increasing interest in topographical prints—and in sporting and coaching prints for which aquatint was extensively used—the situation has changed, and the better examples are fiercely fought for at the major auction rooms.

During the 1830s, aquatint was overtaken by the newer process of lithography for topographical illustration. A study of one of the great catalogues of Major J. R. Abbey's collection, *Scenery of Great Britain and Ireland in Aquatint and Lithography*, gives some idea of the relative popularity of various areas of the British Isles as subjects of illustrations in these media. London heads the list with fifty-one publications devoted to its scenes; other significant towns are Brighton (fifteen), Bath (eleven), Hastings and St Leonards (eleven), Oxford (ten), Cambridge (nine), Windsor (eight), York (eight) and Sidmouth (five). Devonshire leads the counties with eighteen, followed by Yorkshire (sixteen), the Isle of Wight (ten) and Kent (eight). The Lake District scores eleven, but Derbyshire only four. Of rivers, the Thames is featured eight times and the Wye seven, while Wales defeats Scotland twenty-four to fifteen. It is interesting to note the obvious popularity of the South Coast resorts, which during this period became accessible by the railway; the Lake District and Derbyshire no longer dominated tourism as they did at the end of the eighteenth century. Abbey's *Scenery* is a list of books, not of singly issued plates, and it is not entirely comprehensive; within these limitations, however, its authority stands firm. It also gives an indication of those artists and engravers whose work was in most demand by publishers. Twelve men were represented in at least ten different publications: S. Alken, J. Bluck, W. Gauci, J. Hassell, Daniel and Robert Havell, G. Hawkins, F. C. Lewis, A. Pugin, J. C. Stadler, W. Walker and William Westall. The details of over five hundred books are listed; here is richness indeed.

Despite the considerable differences in the processes, Abbey's juxtaposition of aquatint and lithography does have a logical basis. It was the ambition of Charles Hullmandel, arguably the greatest of the lithographic printers working in England, to replace aquatint by lithography for topographical illustration. Up to a point he succeeded; but his success was limited by various factors. Lithography failed to attract enough artists of quality; for many years it was expensive owing to heavy duties payable on the imported stone; and photography moved in on the illustrated book market. For the most part, the lithographers themselves concentrated on trying to reproduce via the stone the techniques and effects of watercolour painting or drawing, and it was not until late in the nineteenth century, notably in the hands of Whistler, that it became used as a means of expression for its own particular merits and qualities.

The story of the invention of lithography by the Bavarian Aloys Senefelder is well enough known. Initially a playwright, Senefelder discovered the method of printing from limestone in 1798, when seeking a cheap way to reproduce the text of his own plays. Johann André, a music publisher, invited him to London in 1800 to take out a patent, which Senefelder sold in the following year to Johann's brother Philip, who opened a lithographic printing house. The process was originally known as 'polyautography', and André published his *Specimens of Polyautography* in 1803, a series of prints drawn on the stone in pen by a number of painters, including West, Stothard and Fuseli. The project was unprofitable, however, and André followed Senefelder back to Germany. Another German, G. J. Vollweiler, took over the firm and published a further collection of prints, but with no more success despite the quality of some of the examples. Vollweiler gave up in 1807, the same year in which the first English lithographic book illustration appeared—a plate by J. T. Smith in *The Antiquities of Westminster*, also in the pen and ink style and, apart from its novelty value, not especially remarkable.

After this unpromising start, little lithographic work was done in England for the next few years. Then in 1813, D. J. Redman set up a lithographic printing-house in Bath, which ran for about three years. Thomas Barker, known as 'Barker of Bath' although he was born in Monmouthshire, a landscape painter who exhibited at the Academy and the British Institute, became interested in drawing on stone and produced two sets of impressions, *Rustic Figures after Nature*, with forty plates, and *Drawings of Landscape Scenery*, with thirty-two plates, in 1813 and 1814. Barker's drawings were made with a pen and at first sight closely resemble etchings. In 1817, the process moved back to London when Ackermann brought it into his repertoire. He used it for some of the plates in the *Repository* and gave the method wide publicity by publishing Senefelder's *Complete Course of Lithography*, not the first instructional manual on the subject but probably the one which had the most influence. Then in 1818, Charles Joseph Hullmandel, the London-born son of a German family, established his own press, partly in order to reproduce his own drawings in lithography. Together with Ackermann he published a treatise, *The Art of Drawing on Stone*, 1824, and three years later a further work, *On Some Important Improvements in Lithographic Printing*.

One advantage of lithography was that the original artist could not only draw the picture but could transfer it on to the stone himself, if he chose, thus dispensing with the services of the engraver. Some of the earlier work in lithographic chalk, a specially made compound which replaced the pen and ink method, is very similar in effect to soft-ground etching, which possibly confused Major Abbey who listed Samuel Prout's *Views of Rural Cottages* as lithographs, although the full title indicates that they were 'drawn and etched in the manner of chalk'. Prout did do lithographic work, but mostly of foreign scenes; he was one of the contributors to the substantial *Britannia Delineata*, published with a text in both English and French in 1822–3 and with plates by the leading practitioners in the craft, James Duffield Harding, William Westall and Hullmandel himself. Another lithographic artist, perhaps the most prolific in the field, was Francis Nicholson, a Yorkshireman, who is said to have produced over eight hundred drawings on stone. Wales, Scotland, Devon and particularly Scarborough in his native county were the areas he delineated most often. Nicholson's work is mostly soft in texture, slightly fuzzy and clearly influenced by picturesque theory.

Westall turned from aquatint to lithography, producing views of the Lakes, Windsor and Edinburgh, and notably *Thirty Five Views on the Thames*—his earlier hunting ground—which appeared in seven instalments beginning in 1821 and as a collected publication in 1824. Harding, a slightly younger man, was a pupil of Samuel Prout and was also for a time apprenticed to the line engraver James Pye. He was something of a prodigy, exhibiting a picture at the Academy at the age of thirteen. He worked for Hullmandel, making the lithographs after originals by J. F. Lewis, David Roberts and Clarkson Stanfield. He was also responsible for *Subjects from the Works of the late R. P. Bonington*, who died in 1828 at the early age of twenty-seven after a brief but brilliant career mainly spent in France and Italy.

Harding produced three collections of lithographs from his own drawings, including several English topographical views, namely *Sketches from Home and Abroad*, with fifty plates, published 1836, *Harding's Portfolio* of twenty-four views, 1837, and *The Park and the Forest*, 1841. In this last work, which was intended 'to illustrate the picturesque beauty of trees themselves, alone and in combination', all the twenty-six plates were produced by lithotint. Harding repeated several of his designs in his own instructional drawing books, such as

The Principals and Practice of Art, *Lessons on Art* and *Elementary Art*, all of which included many lithographs as well as engraved and etched plates. Lithotint was a method in which a brush was used to coat the stone with different shades of lithographic ink in an attempt, often quite successful, to reproduce the effect of watercolour. *The Park and the Forest*, which was printed on Smith & Chapman's 'Adhesed Paper', mounted in the same way as India paper, appeared without text in an issue of one thousand copies. It was much admired by Ruskin, who was one of Harding's pupils. Seven years before, Hullmandel had printed another set of lithographs of trees, *Studies of Trees with and without Foliage*, by Miss S. A. Young. Unlike lady etchers, lady lithographers are seldom met with. According to the list of subscribers in this volume, about a hundred and thirty copies were printed, India paper proofs costing two guineas and the ordinary version £1 6s. Harding must have known Miss Young's work but no record of their meeting has so far been traced. Later in his career Harding made many coloured lithographs for J. P. Lawson's *Scotland Delineated*, a collection of views after some of the most popular painters of the time, including George Cattermole, David Roberts and W. L. Leitch, published in parts between 1847 and 1854.

Lithography was not greatly used for book illustration; the majority of topographical lithographs were published in sets in paper wrappers and without text, or in portfolios or volume form. London continued to dominate the quality trade, with Hullmandel setting the pace, but other firms gradually began producing work of comparable quality. The Belgian, Louis Haghe, came to London after studying the subject and joined forces with the printer William Day. Aided by a well-trained staff, Day and Haghe produced some excellent prints, with Haghe transferring the original drawing on to the stone and Day being responsible for the printing. The firm, which became Lithographers to the Queen, was known as Day & Son from 1852, later becoming Vincent Brooks, Day & Son. Other leading lithographic houses included Englemann and C. Graf, who eventually combined into Englemann, Graf, Conde & Co. Newman & Co was another London firm which printed lithographs for local publishers, unhelpfully often omitting the names of the lithographers themselves. Dickinson & Co, E. Gambart and Hanhart are also names that frequently recur.

Local views were often printed in London but published locally. Most country towns seemed to have their own publishers in the 1840s and 1850s; a random check produces the names of publishers in Bath, Eton, Exeter, Bristol, Winchester, Hereford, Dover, Maidstone, Ramsgate, Oxford, Liverpool, Wells, Walsall, Guildford, Brighton, Chichester, St Leonards, Warwick,

Plate 33 Chirk Aqueduct, from a drawing by George Pickering, lithographed by Englemann & Co and published by J. Seacombe of Chester. Pickering was a drawing-master in Chester and was well known for his views of Lancashire and Cheshire

Malvern, Scarborough, Whitby and York. J. Seacombe of Chester published G. Pickering's splendid drawings of the Chirk and Pontcysyllte aqueducts, printed in London by Englemann (Plate 33). Barnstaple was served by Mrs Wildman's Repository; E. Turle's view of the town was lithographed by Haghe and printed by Day (Plate 34). But some work was entirely locally produced; George Rowe, himself both painter and lithographer, printed and published much of his own work, first at Exeter and later in Cheltenham. Another Devonshire artist, William Spreat, operated in a similar way, publishing sets of prints sometimes over his own imprint of Spreat and Norman and sometimes conjointly with a London house. He produced about two hundred lithographs, although not all were after his own originals. In view of its comparative cheapness, the large number of reproductions possible and the ease of retouching the stone, compared with the labour of re-engraving a plate, lithography became a good commercial proposition—even if it did involve the heavy labour of dragging around large blocks of stone. If you could draw, and you could employ the services of a printer, you could make a lithograph, and quickly too. The result was that a great deal of mediocre work was produced, much of it to satisfy the tourist trade, and its interest is historical rather than artistic—rather like the interest in picture postcards of the 1920s. But it is also worth mentioning that lithography had a pronounced effect on the development of the science of geology. The series of *Transactions of the Geological Society of London* that began in 1824 was illustrated by George Scharf's drawings lithographed by Hullmandel. The substitution of lithography for engravings improved the accuracy of the illustrations and enabled a large number of pictures to be published at a comparatively low cost.

George Scharf was also a topographical draughtsman and was interested in the construction of the London to Birmingham railway. His illustrations may have helped to show the way to the young John Cooke Bourne, who had studied engraving under John Pye and was encouraged by John Britton to make sketches of the railway excavations at the London end of the line. So successful were the sketches that Britton thought them worthy of publication, suggesting lithography as the reproductive medium. Although best known as an antiquarian, Britton also responded to the achievements of the new industrial age and in 1833 published five thousand copies of his own *Lecture on Railways, particularly the line from London to Bristol*, which he had given at the British Institution. In 1838 the first number of Bourne's *Series of Lithographed Drawings on the London and Birmingham Railway* was published by Bourne and Ackermann for one guinea; the second part appeared a few months later, and the last two parts, with a descriptive account of the railway by Britton, came out in the following year. Then the four parts were issued in a single volume, *Drawings of the London and Birmingham Railway* was published by Bourne and Ackermann thirty-six illustrations. The reviews were favourable and the names of several discerning subscribers have been recorded, but the publication did not prove a financial success. Francis Klingender suggested that 'the art patrons of the day wished for anything rather than to be reminded of the social and technological revolution going on all around them.' And it does seem that the early Victorians, intrigued by railways though they may have been, wanted to look at pictures of cows rather than of trains, and preferred ruins to excavations.

For the most part, Bourne's buff-tinted plates are confidently and powerfully

Plate 34 (*overleaf*) View of Barnstaple, drawn by E. Turle, lithographed by Louis Haghe, printed by W. Day in London and published at Mrs Wildman's Repository, Barnstaple, about 1830. It is a typical example of the very many locally published lithographs of this period

Plate 35 Blasting rocks at Linslade, lithograph by John Cooke Bourne from his *Drawings of the London and Birmingham Railway*, 1839. This plate shows something of the violence inflicted by railway construction on the countryside—note the folk fleeing in terror, left centre

composed. Their topographic interest lies in their depiction of the changes the railway was making, or had already made, in the countryside through which it passed. They show the great cuttings and embankments, the tunnels under construction, the bridges and viaducts and the solid, triumphant stations of Euston and Birmingham (Plate 35). 'Under his lucid eye', wrote Klingender, 'the railway cut like a lash across the face of the countryside that his contemporaries, such as James Duffield Harding, Samuel Prout and William Leitch liked to populate with noble, unhurried peasants, pursuing their simple tasks in idyllic surroundings.' The only peasants that Bourne shows are running away from the noise and smoke of the rock-blasting at Linslade; otherwise the figures in his drawings are men at work, the engineers and navvies of the early years of the Railway Age. Among the most impressive feats—and the reference is to both engineering and lithography—are the cuttings at Blisworth and Tring, the Avon viaduct, and the construction of Kilsby tunnel. The monumental studies of the entrances to the terminal stations, Euston and Curzon Street, Birmingham, are other splendid examples.

Bourne's second great series of lithographs, the *History and Description of the Great Western Railway*, appeared in volume form in 1846, sponsored and printed by Charles Cheffins, who shared Bourne's interest in railways and printing, and published by David Bogue of Fleet Street. Whereas the London and Birmingham Railway was shown during construction, the illustrations for the Great Western line from London to Bristol show the details of working practice. The volume itself, with its striking frontispiece of the locomotive *Acheron* emerging from a tunnel, is remarkable not only for its plates but also for the reflection it gives of the concerns of its time. The introduction is packed with information about the history, engineering and topography of the line, as was to be expected. There are maps, cross-sections of gradients and other relevant material, and a study of the geology of Bristol. But the book also contains a lengthy section of Church notes, and a further series of lithographs, also by Bourne, of some of the churches and their monuments in the vicinity of the line. The railway—and its stations, tunnels, bridges, inclines and associated buildings—is depicted in thirty-six illustrations and in many of them it already seems an integral part of the landscape. The fine illustrations show the Great Western in those early years when, with its broad gauge laid out by Isambard Kingdom Brunel and its inborn pride, it was almost a law unto itself. It has been noted that 'the significance of these plates is indicated by their regular reproduction in the best standard and official histories of the company, as well as in the "popular" and "hack" books about the line.'

Brunel's great railway even improved the landscape, as seen through Bourne's eyes anyway. Look at the 'View from above Box Tunnel', where the distant line leads the eye into the centre of the picture. See how the embankment forms a protective arm around the town of Chippenham, and how, in another plate, the central arch of the viaduct provides a frame for the view of the town and a shelter for the sheep and cattle. St James's bridge and station add a dimension to Bath (Plate 36); the Wharncliffe viaduct dramatically dominates the placid scenery of Hanwell. Box tunnel and the Long tunnel in Fox's Wood are engineering triumphs beautifully scaled to the surrounding landscape. And number two tunnel, near Bristol, strikes the picturesque note

Plate 36 (overleaf) St James' Bridge and Station, Bath. Bourne's *Great Western Railway* was printed by C. F. Cheffins and published by Daniel Bogue in 1846

previously referred to. To quote from the text: 'During the progress of the works the hill side came down into the excavation, and rendered the proposed support useless, the work was accordingly left in its incomplete state, and the accident produced a very serviceable, and a picturesque tunnel front.'

Bourne's work is exceptional. For railway devotees it is rivalled possibly only by Bury's coloured aquatints, mentioned above, and a very rare trio of hand-coloured lithographs, *Illustrations of the Great Western and Bristol & Exeter Railways*, which first appeared in or about 1835 and were reprinted in 1840. They were drawn on stone by Haghe, after drawings by W. W. Young. While they lack the confidence and compositional skill of Bourne's designs, they have their own unique nostalgic charm. It seems likely that they were intended as part of a larger series which, for some unknown reason, was discontinued. Arthur F. Tait drew and lithographed two sets of views: the Manchester and Leeds Railway, and the London and North Western. They are not without interest, but do not have the quality of the other work described.

By its nature, lithography was able to give an impression of immediacy which other reproductive methods available at the time—with the possible exception of soft-ground etching—were unable to provide. This can be seen in the great collection of lithographs by Thomas Shotter Boys entitled *Original Views of London As It Is*, published by Boys himself, who was at the time Printseller to the Royal Family, in 1842. This was the successor to his coloured lithographs, *Picturesque Architecture in Paris, Ghent, Antwerp, Rouen*, etc, which had appeared three years earlier, each plate printed by Hullmandel in colour from a series of stones, a method which Boys claimed to have invented. The *Picturesque Views* rival—many would say surpass—the best of the aquatints in reproducing the subtle effects of watercolour, but the weight of stone that had to be heaved about to produce the plates in their full glory was enormous, and the enterprise was extremely costly. For his London views Boys used two stones for each plate, one bearing the outline and the other the washes of buff tint. Single plates were mounted on card and hand-coloured, but the original publication in volume form was left plain. Of this collection, Abbey wrote 'it records London at a period when good pictorial records were few. The London of the 1840s is probably more difficult to reconstruct than that of any other period in the nineteenth century. High production costs and changing fashion was causing the aquatint to die out: photography was still in the experimental stage, and chromos did not appear until 1850.'

The *Original Views of London* were printed by Hullmandel and carried a descriptive text in English and French by Charles Ollier. The Thames is busy,

Plate 37 London from Greenwich, a lithograph from Thomas Shotter Boys' *Original Views of London As It Is*, 1842. On the left is the Royal Observatory and in the centre the Naval Asylum and Hospital. The dome of St Paul's can be seen on the skyline

people bustle about or stop to chat, there are traffic jams and the roads seem to be under repair as often as they are today. Two balloons float above Piccadilly, water pipes are being laid, ladies run to catch an omnibus, and in one plate the artist himself stands plumb in the centre, sketching the scene before him. And see how many carts, posters, signs and statues there are bearing the name T. S. Boys! In his depiction of London buildings, Boys is at least the equal of Pugin in Ackermann's major publications. Among the most impressive plates are the distant view of London from Greenwich, with the Hospital in the centre and the Observatory to the left (Plate 37); the 'Entry to the Strand from Charing Cross'—a year before Nelson's Column was erected; 'Piccadilly Looking Towards the City'; 'Mansion House, Cheapside'; and 'Hyde Park Corner', where, to quote the text, 'every object that meets the eye is stately,

Plate 38 (*overleaf*) Hyde Park Corner, lithograph from Thomas Shotter Boys' *Original Views of London As It Is*, 1842. 'Every object that meets the eye is stately, graceful, courtly and metro-politan.' There is a sixpenny omnibus in the centre and the road, as usual, is under repair

graceful, courtly and metropolitan' (Plate 38). Boys had studied in Paris with the brilliant watercolourist Richard Parkes Bonington, and had learned engraving from George Cooke to whom he was articled at the age of fourteen. He was born in 1803, a year after Bonington, and died in 1874. His lithographic work is brilliant; perhaps there is no other English lithographer to whom this adjective could be applied. What is odd is that there are so few references to him in standard works on British Art, though you can discover plenty of mediocrities without having to look far. Martin Hardie says that as a painter Boys was neglected, and that for a living he had to turn to hack work as an engraver and etcher. Ruskin employed him but seems not to have praised him publicly, 'and he passed into oblivion'. Fate plays its own game, however, and today you may have to pay more for a lithograph by Boys than for 'an original watercolour' by many of his contemporary artists so much more highly regarded in their own time.

Bourne's railways, Boys' London—these mark the peaks of achievement in British topographical lithography of the middle years of the nineteenth century. Other works that rise above the average include the many coloured lithographs by J. Arnout, published by E. Gambart & Co about 1855; these are careful and accurate views of London and several provincial towns and cities, that of Newcastle upon Tyne being of particular interest and quality. Some of the more pleasing views of the Lake District were lithographed by T. Picken after the drawings of J. B. Pyne and published by Day & Son, 1859. Good Scottish views include two sets by Samuel Swarbreck, *Sketches in Scotland*, with twenty-five tinted lithographs, and *Views of Edinburgh*, both published in 1839, and *Scotland Delineated*, by J. P. Lawson, which we have already mentioned. Among the better Welsh views are the tinted lithographs by T. C. Dibdin of *The Waterfalls of Caernarvonshire* and George Hawkins' pictures of the Menai, Britannia and Conway bridges, some of them tinted and some hand-coloured, published by Catherall of Chester about 1850.

At times one is surprised by the subjects chosen by lithographers or publishers. Liverpool does not seem a likely subject for a series of *Picturesque Views* as late as 1864, but nevertheless W. Herdman found it so and earlier in the century Richard Ayton thought it the second most beautiful town. And the proud citizens of Maidstone were delighted with J. W. C. Williams' tinted lithograph of their new amenity as depicted in his *Perspective View of Public Baths and Wash-Houses* that appeared about 1845.

4

LINE ENGRAVING ON STEEL

The first British steel engraver is mentioned in Pigot's *London Directory* for 1822 which also lists 179 copper engravers, sixteen lithographic printers and thirty-eight printsellers. The following year, Thomas Lupton was awarded a medal by the Society of Arts for the engraving of a mezzotint on steel. The advantages of steel soon became obvious; the plates could withstand several thousand impressions, not merely a few hundred, before showing signs of wear, and the metal was no more difficult to work. Within a few years the publishers were turning to steel, and a host of little 'Annuals' appeared in the late 1820s and 1830s; *The Literary Souvenir*, *The Keepsake*, *The Amulet*, *The Bijou*, *Friendship's Offering* and *The Remembrance* are the names of just a few. John Britton ascribed the financial failure of his *Picturesque Antiquities of English Cities* mostly to the substitution of steel for copper. This publication, with sixty copper engravings and twenty-three woodcuts, sold in volume form in the cheapest size for £7 4s, but—as Britton later said—'the age of cheap literature had commenced, and the circulation of the volume was very much less than the proprietors had expected.' In fact, it failed to cover its costs, even after the plates and copyright were auctioned off. 'Though the best-written and illustrated of all his works, and altogether an interesting volume, the *Picturesque Antiquities of English Cities* has proved the most losing speculation the author ever embarked in', wrote the disappointed Britton.

It is not always easy to distinguish between later copper- and earlier steel-engraved work, but steel permitted closer ruling than copper, as well as greater detail in a smaller space. The copper engravers could work on steel with equal facility, or equal labour, so that men like Willmore, Miller and Wallis were engraving after Turner on both metals during the same period, the larger copper engravings for the major prestige publications and the smaller steel

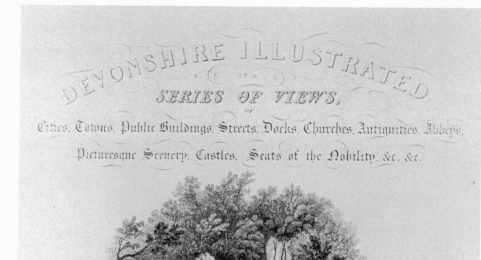

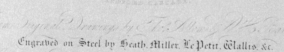

Plate 39 Title-page of *Devonshire Illustrated*, published 1829. The original drawings were by Thomas Allom and W. H. Bartlett, and the engravers included Heath, Miller, Le Petit and Wallis. The vignette shows Lydford Cascade

engravings for the Annuals or book-illustration vignettes. But there has been plenty of confusion between copper and steel plates. It is helpful to remember that if the plate first appeared before 1822 then it is almost certainly copper, and if there is evidence of a large print-run then it is likely to be steel. Imports of copper were affected by the Napoleonic Wars with a consequent effect on copper engraving, but the trade did revive to some extent in later years and much work was done on steel-coated copper plates. Both copper and steel plates also changed hands from time to time, when printers and publishers sold up and went out of business for whatever reason, and might be reused years later, sometimes tidied up or altered to keep pace with changes of buildings or fashion, sometimes in their original condition. It is also worth noting that with steel engravings the various proof states ceased to have any particular significance, there being no noticeable difference between the first and five thousandth impression taken.

Sometimes, however, the publishers were positively helpful. T. Allen's *New and Complete History of the County of York*, in three volumes 1828–31, is considerately described on the title-page as 'Illustrated by a Series of Views, engraved on Steel from original Drawings by Nathaniel Whittock'. These volumes contain 152 engravings, most of them by J. Rogers and J. Shury. Some of them are ascribed not to an individual but to a firm, Fenner, Sears & Co. Mudie's *Hampshire*, Gastineau's *Wales Illustrated*, Tombleson's *Thames and Medway* and Roscoe's *London and Birmingham Railway* are among other publications where 'steel' is specifically mentioned on the title-page. After 1830, nearly all the line-engraved work was done on steel, but the odd mistake in distinguishing between the two media does not greatly matter (Plate 39).

By the time steel engraving was becoming popular, the influence of picturesque theory was diminishing. The adjective still appeared in titles from time to time: for example, Tillotson's *Picturesque Scenery in Wales*, published in 1860. But the emphasis was shifting to the accurate, detailed view, no longer necessarily framed in foliage or deliberately roughed up. It is true that the views selected were pleasant views, whether rural or metropolitan; it was left to a foreign artist, Gustave Doré, to show the less acceptable side of the results of Victorian economic progress, as it had been left to the caricaturists Gillray and Cruikshank to show the less acceptable side of political and social life. Sometimes the plates illustrated books of purely local interest, like C. Mackie's *Historical Description of the Abbey and Town of Paisley*, a volume of 170 pages with five engravings after his own drawings by Joseph Swan, or J. Train's *Historical and Statistical Account of the Isle of Man*, published in two volumes, 1845, totalling 789 pages, brightened up with two maps and three engravings by W. H. Lizars. There were county histories, such as Hutchins' *Dorset*, which appeared in four massive volumes illustrated by over a hundred engravings, some on copper but over half of them by J. H. Le Keux on steel. Other large-scale county studies included Baines' *History of the County Palatine and Duchy of Lancaster*, his *Lancashire and Cheshire*, and his *Yorkshire Past and Present*, all worthy and substantial works. The two volumes of Wright's *History and Topography of the County of Essex* contained over one and a half thousand pages of text and more than one hundred engravings, almost all of them after drawings by the prolific W. H. Bartlett.

In these examples—and there are many more which could be added—the illustrations were subservient to the text, and generally speaking, these were not the volumes which later generations broke up for the sake of the plates. Books whose plates formed their *raison d'être*, with perhaps one or two pages of descriptive text for each plate or sometimes no text at all, were the ones most commonly broken up. Such were Rose's various collections of views of the northern counties, published in the 1830s and '40s, with most of the engravings after drawings by Thomas Allom. Allom was an architect, a designer of churches, workhouses and a military asylum, but he found time to produce an enormous number of views, mainly in Westmorland, Cumberland, Northumberland and Durham (Plate 40). The three volumes devoted to these counties contained 215 plates, nearly all of them after Allom with a few after Gastineau and Pickering. Thomas Hosmer Shepherd was another popular illustrator; his *London and its Environs in the Nineteenth Century* comprised 192 plates and his *Metropolitan Improvements . . . displayed in a Series of Engravings . . . from Original Drawings, taken from the Objects themselves expressly for this Work* contained a further 159. He also made 101 drawings of Edinburgh for *Modern Athens* and was the major contributor to Britton's *Bath and Bristol*, with Bartlett and J. P. Neale. With the exception of the last named, all of these first appeared in monthly parts, published by Jones (Plate 41). Each number cost one shilling; if we remember that Britton's *Picturesque Antiquities*, which was appearing at the same time as *Metropolitan Improvements*, cost twenty-four shillings a number, we can appreciate the comment that 'the age of cheap literature had commenced'. Between 1826 and 1831, Shepherd made well over four hundred drawings for the engravers, over forty of whom worked on his London scenes and most of whom he must have known well. His surviving drawings and watercolours show him to have been an accurate observer and a firm draughtsman, with a good sense of composition. Gilpin, we remember, described canals as 'disgusting'; what would he have thought of Shepherd's *Picturesque Tour on the Regent's Canal*, a set of six large aquatints published in

Plate 40 Kendal from the Castle, steel engraving by W. Le Petit after an original drawing by Thomas Allom, 1832. This plate appeared in T. Rose's *Westmorland, Cumberland, Durham and Northumberland Illustrated*, and was used again in Allom and Rose's *The British Switzerland*, 1858. Thomas Allom (1804–72) was an architect as well as a prolific illustrator, a careful draughtsman whose work was well suited to reproduction by steel engraving

1825? The originals were used a few years later in *Metropolitan Improvements* and one of them, 'The Double Lock & East Entrance to the Islington Tunnel', engraved by F. J. Havell, must today be the best known and most frequently reproduced of all nineteenth-century canal scenes. Havell also engraved the view of the City Basin and several other plates. Wallis, Deeble, Higham, Henshall, Barber, Tombleson, Tingle and Watkins were among those who engraved after Shepherd, and the level of their achievement, considering the speed at which it is clear they had to work, was remarkably high.

As we have seen, William Westall provided several notable subjects for aquatint and lithography. In 1830, Charles Tilt of Fleet Street published *Great Britain Illustrated*, containing 118 views after Westall engraved 'by and under the direction of' Edward Finden. This volume, which carried two plates a page with brief descriptions by Thomas Moule, reappeared as two octavo volumes,

The Landscape Album, first and second series, 1832 and 1834. The preface shows that since the introduction of steel—and with the more settled conditions abroad—changes had taken place. 'This Volume', said the publishers, 'is presented to the Public under a conviction that a Series of Views, taken from our native country, will be at least as favourably received as if the talents of the eminent Artists engaged in their production had been employed in portraying the beauties of a foreign land.' The publishers found it surprising that the English, while anxiously searching after the picturesque on the Continent, 'neglect comparatively their own beautiful and interesting Island, many parts of which . . . are equal if not superior to any scenery to be found abroad. The great commercial cities too . . . should, it is presumed, be regarded with peculiar interest by every true lover of his country.' The *Landscape Album* volumes were designed 'to please all classes of society' and were priced to be 'generally accessible'. To judge by the number of engravings from these volumes that can be found today, mostly recently hand-coloured, the editions must have been large ones.

Edward Finden engraved about half of Westall's views, the others being by Edward Francis, James Fife, John Roffe, S. Rawle and J. Stubbs. Some of the views are what might be described as 'modified picturesque' but there are a few surprises including an almost Turneresque view of Sheffield and a picture of Preston from the north, dominated by windmills, and described in the text by Thomas Moule as 'the most fashionable town in the county'. One of the most desirable places in which to live at the time would appear to have been Salford, the Crescent with the river Irwell and the distant hills forming a 'picture which never fails to create admiration'. The less presentable sides of life are, naturally, omitted.

Nationwide coverage, as in *Great Britain Illustrated*, was not very frequent, few artists being as fond of mobility as Westall. A specially fine example of a collection of local views that did not concentrate, as was usual practice, on architecture is the *Scenery of the Rivers of Norfolk*, after paintings by James Stark, published in 1834. Stark was a pupil of Crome and a member of the Norwich Society of Artists; he exhibited at the leading London galleries and, after Crome and Cotman, ranks among the best of the Norfolk painters. He began this particular series of paintings in 1827, 'designed to illustrate an undertaking which was about to re-open an ancient harbour', as he said in his dedication to William IV. The undertaking was the Norwich and Lowestoft Navigation, which to some extent re-established Norwich as an inland port. Stark's views of the Yare, Bure and Waveney show the scenery and activities of the rivers and riversides; they are detailed, lively and attractively composed.

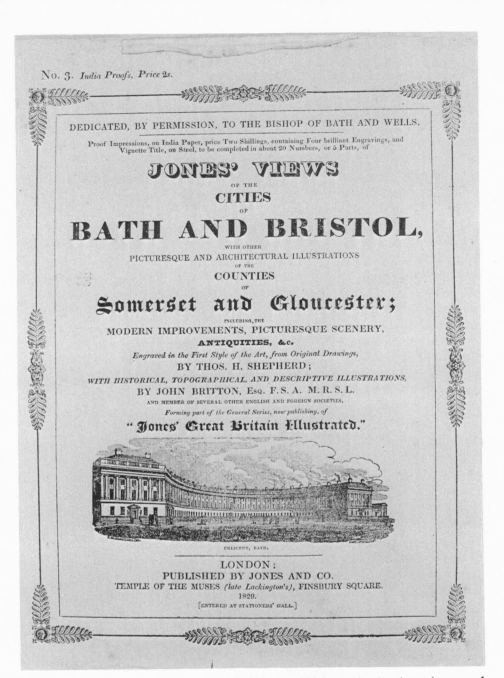

DEDICATED, BY PERMISSION, TO THE BISHOP OF BATH AND WELLS.

Proof Impressions, on India Paper, price Two Shillings, containing Four brilliant Engravings, and Vignette Title, on Steel, to be completed in about 20 Numbers, or 5 Parts, of

JONES' VIEWS

OF THE

CITIES

OF

BATH AND BRISTOL,

WITH OTHER

PICTURESQUE AND ARCHITECTURAL ILLUSTRATIONS

OF THE

COUNTIES

OF

Somerset and Gloucester;

INCLUDING THE

MODERN IMPROVEMENTS, PICTURESQUE SCENERY,

ANTIQUITIES, &c.

Engraved in the First Style of the Art, from Original Drawings,

BY THOS. H. SHEPHERD;

WITH HISTORICAL, TOPOGRAPHICAL, AND DESCRIPTIVE ILLUSTRATIONS,

BY JOHN BRITTON, Esq. F.S.A. M.R.S.L.

AND MEMBER OF SEVERAL OTHER ENGLISH AND FOREIGN SOCIETIES.

Forming part of the General Series, now publishing, of

"Jones' Great Britain Illustrated."

CRESCENT, BATH.

LONDON;

PUBLISHED BY JONES AND CO.

TEMPLE OF THE MUSES *(late Lackington's)*, FINSBURY SQUARE.

1829.

[ENTERED AT STATIONERS' HALL.]

Plate 41 Printed wrapper of number 3 of Jones' *Views of the Cities of Bath and Bristol*, engraved from drawings by Thomas Hosmer Shepherd with text by John Britton. India proofs of four engravings cost two shillings

The best of the contemporary engravers were employed, among them many of Turner's interpreters including Miller, Goodall, Radclyffe, Brandard, Varrall and George and W. J. Cooke. Miller's engraving of Carrow Bridge is especially fine, and there is a beautiful vignette of the entrance to Oulton Dyke, engraved by W. Forrest. The plates were accompanied by an informative text by J. W. Robberds. Among the subscribers, in addition to the king, were two dukes, two earls, two bishops, a viscount and sundry other members of the peerage as well as Cotman, Crome and Constable. Yet the work, according to Samuel Redgrave, 'notwithstanding its great merit and interest, produced no adequate reward.' Possibly it was too expensive to sell widely; possibly the interest was too localised. But the plates must stand amongst the best of the line-engraved work of the nineteenth century.

Another collection of river scenes, Tombleson's *Thames*, appeared in the same year. Its full title is *Eighty Picturesque Views on the Thames and Medway, engraved on Steel by the First Artists*; there is a historical description of each view by W. G. Fearnside and all the plates except one are after Tombleson's own drawings (Plate 42). William Tombleson appears in various guises; he was both original artist and publisher, but he was also an engraver whose work is often met with. The attraction of the Thames and Medway plates is partly due to their decorative surrounds; as an artist Tombleson does not compare with Stark. He is competent but not imaginative, and does not seem to have shown his paintings at any of the principal London exhibitions. The captions to his plates are in French and German as well as English, indicating that he hoped for continental sales. Most of his engravers seem to have been recruited from the second eleven, as it were, with few of the leading practitioners represented. There are two plates by Varrall and one by Jeavons, but about half are by H. Winkles, one of the half dozen or so of that surname working about this time. Nevertheless, Tombleson's *Thames* remains a volume greatly in demand and the single plates, especially of the bridges, are very popular.

Like the Thames, the southern coast was a frequent subject of nineteenth-century illustration. Ten years after Turner's *Southern Coast*, Smith Elder & Co published Stanfield's *Coast Scenery: A Series of Views in the British Channel*, from original drawings taken expressly for the work by Clarkson Stanfield, RA. Stanfield served in the Navy; following an accident he was discharged and became a scene-painter in London, soon gaining fame for his work at Drury Lane. He also painted and exhibited marine views, and was elected to the Royal Academy in 1835. *Coast Scenery* was published in the following year, dedicated—like Stark's book—to William IV. There are forty plates, a few of them of the Normandy coast and Guernsey, by the best of the contemporary

Plate 42 Sunbury Locks, from *Eighty Picturesque Views on the Thames and Medway*, drawn by W. Tombleson and published by him in 1834. This plate was engraved by W. Lacey

engravers: Miller, Goodall, Cousen, Kernot, Brandard; the Cookes and the Findens among them. Stanfield himself was a workmanlike painter, 'an honest craftsman' Martin Hardie called him. Dickens liked him and admired his work, and the engravers—especially those who had laboured under Turner—applied themselves to remarkable effect in these small plates, measuring only five and a half by three and a half inches. Among the outstanding plates are Cousen's 'Falmouth', the view dominated by a receiving-ship, Allen's 'Dartmouth' and

127

Miller's 'Botallack Mine, Cornwall', but all are good.

Following *Coast Scenery* came the two volumes known as Finden's *Ports and Harbours*. The first volume appeared in 1838, published by Charles Tilt and containing forty-nine plates. It reappeared in 1842, extended to sixty-five plates and with a second volume including a further fifty-nine, now published by George Virtue. Two of the best marine painters of the century, George Balmer and Edward William Cooke, were among the artists of Volume I, which also contained work by Thomas Creswick and J. D. Harding and three or four other contributors (Plate 43). The remaining plates in the second issue of the first volume, and all those in the second, were after W. H. Bartlett and are typical of his competent but undistinguished work. The Finden brothers, Edward and William, did most of the engraving of the first set of plates, but the Bartlett views were engraved by a host of others, including Brandard, Higham, Varrall, Wallis, Mossman and Armytage.

In the edition published by Virtue, the name of Bartlett takes precedence, a position deserved by quantity rather than quality. In the 1874 edition he still ranks first, followed by Harding and Creswick; there is no mention of Balmer and Cooke on the title-page. *Ports and Harbours* was a popular publication, but it is strange that it was thought worth reprinting so late in the century when it must have seemed curiously old-fashioned. Somehow it is rather a depressing collection, lacking the unity of Stanfield's vision; the *Coastal Scenery* plates, although smaller, have more impact and are worked with more brilliance.

J. P. Anderson's *Book of British Topography*, first published in 1881, lists nearly fourteen thousand volumes, the contents of the British topographical section of the British Museum library, where Anderson worked as an attendant. Although it is not comprehensive, it is still a very valuable work of reference and includes the illustrated books which were published with text. More pages are devoted to London and its surrounding area than to any other part of the British Isles except Scotland. One of the outstanding steel-engraved illustrated books in this section is W. E. Trotter's *Select Illustrated Topography of Thirty Miles around London*, published in 1839. This contains thirty-five engravings, most of them by W. and J. Henshall—the book is also known as *Henshall's Illustrated Topography*—and the others by Varrall, Floyd, Bentley and Mottram, after drawings by Charles Marshall, J. W. Allen, G. B. Campion and a few other contemporaries.

Trotter's prose style can be described as 'early Victorian verbose', and perhaps we should pause to enjoy a sample. 'In the earlier stages of society, ere the cloud of superstitition had been dispelled by the sunlight of truth, and when oral tradition was almost the sole vehicle of information, it is not surprising that every object of historical interest should have been invested with the veil of romance.' The engravings themselves are much more explicit. There is a hint or two of the picturesque and a few Turneresque skies, but there are also many features of contemporary interest. The plate of 'Westminster from Chelsea Fields' by Varrall after Marshall shows the Abbey, various churches and the dome of St Paul's in the distance. In the middle distance, however, we have less romantic objects, the gas-works and part of the Millbank penitentiary. The foreground is even more interesting, showing as it does what was left of the old fields that once lay between the metropolis and the village of Chelsea. These fields were being levelled for housing, and in the plate we see 'the machinery and process of the work which is rapidly going on for their complete annihilation.'

Many of the views in the *Illustrated Topography* show the traditional tourist scenes within reach of London, such as Windsor Castle and Hampton Court. Others show less expected beauty spots, like Tottenham Mills and Barking Church. There is a lively view of Twickenham Ait, showing the crowded steampacket *Diamond* moving in to let the summer visitors disembark. And one plate shows the new industrial London: Chalk Farm Bridge over the Birmingham Railway, with a train of carriages heading for Birmingham in the foreground, and chimneys, the engine-house and the 'masses of buildings forming Camden and Kentish towns, Holloway, and Islington' in the middle and further distance. But the view is framed with trees; the spirit of the picturesque just survives.

The leading steel engravers were employed on a major Scottish collection of views, *Scotland Illustrated*, published by George Virtue in 1838. This is also found under an alternative title, *Caledonia Illustrated*. William Beattie contributed the text, and the plates, described as 'engraved under the direction of Robert Wallis', were by Varrall, the Cousens, Willmore, Sands, Brandard and many others. The ubiquitous Allom and Bartlett produced most of the drawings and the results are what might be expected—generally competent but not impressive. Some editions contain 168 plates, others rather fewer. Beattie, Virtue and several of the engravers also collaborated on two series of *The Castles and Abbeys of England*, 1844–5; all twenty-seven plates in the second

Plate 43 (*overleaf*) Hastings (view on the beach) from Finden's *Ports and Harbours*. The steel engraving is by E. Finden after a drawing by George Howse. Most of the drawings in this collection were by W. H. Bartlett, and this is Howse's only contribution. He was a member of the Institute of Water-Colour Painters, specialising in landscape and coastal scenes, and he exhibited a large number of pictures from 1837 onwards. He died in 1861

series were after Bartlett, although he did not draw any for the first, and less illustrated, volume.

Robert Wallis was one of the engravers employed on Sir Walter Scott's *Provincial Antiquities and Picturesque Scenery of Scotland*—a successor to his copper-engraved *Border Antiquities*—along with Goodall, Miller, Henry Le Keux, G. Cooke, and others. Turner contributed several drawings, as did Alexander Nasmyth, Calcott, Thomson and Blore. Published in 1826, this was one of the earliest of the steel-engraved Scottish publications. One of the latest, published in 1860 and taking Scott's own writings as its theme, was *An Album of Scottish Scenery*. Places of interest mentioned in Scott's poems and novels were illustrated by leading painters such as Turner, Clarkson Stanfield, Harding, William Westall, Peter de Wint, Cattermole, David Roberts and G. F. Robson, with the Findens, the Cookes, Miller, Radclyffe and Fisher in the list of engravers. John Tillotson wrote the descriptive text, as he did for three companion volumes all published by Allman in London about the same time: *The Beauties of English Scenery, Picturesque Scenery in Wales*, and another Scott work, *The New Waverley Album*, all twenty-five plates of which were engraved by W. Finden. Many of the plates in these volumes had already been used in other publications.

Scotland produced its own engravers, among whom Joseph Swan and William Home Lizars are notable. Swan ran a publishing house in Glasgow and himself made the forty-two engravings of *Select Views on the River Clyde* after drawings by J. Fleming. He drew, engraved and published two books by C. Mackie—historical descriptions of Paisley and Dundee. Lizars was also a painter and engraver, perhaps more accomplished than Swan. His father, Daniel, was an engraver and William Lizars made a good start as an artist, exhibiting two paintings at the Royal Academy in 1812, both of which were engraved. His father's death left him with a large family to support, forcing him to turn to the engraving trade to ensure a regular income. He did the first ten plates for Audubon's *Birds of America* and worked on many publications, including Dibdin's awkwardly titled *Bibliographical Antiquarian and Picturesque Tour in the Northern Counties of England and in Scotland, The Monastic Annals of Teviotdale*, for which he was both engraver and publisher, Oliver and Boyd's *Scottish Tourist Guide to Edinburgh*, and *A Week at Bridge of Allan*, which he also published and which ran to at least six editions. Most Scottish of Scottish productions, however, was probably the single plate 'The Highland Whiskey Still', described in *The Art Union* of October 1839 as 'engraved in the most finished line manner by Robert Graves, Esq, ARA, from the very perfect picture painted by Edwin Landseer, Esq, RA, for His Grace the Duke of

Wellington, KG'. This, published by Hodgson & Graves, His Majesty's Printsellers and Publishers in Ordinary (considering the date was 1839 the reference to *His* Majesty seems odd), was no cheap edition; prints ranged in price from two to eight guineas at the top of the range 'before Letters'.

Wales was the subject of one of the earliest books with steel engravings: *Welsh Scenery*, published by Murray in London, 1823, illustrated with thirty-five plates by Edward Finden from drawings by Captain Robert Batty. Batty was a professional soldier, eventually becoming a lieutenant-colonel in the Grenadiers, and an amateur artist; he served in France, Spain and at Waterloo and published illustrations of his campaigns and his travels abroad. The art historian Samuel Redgrave thought highly of him: 'his industry was great, his works carefully and truthfully drawn, his architecture correct in its proportions and outlines, and his merits as a topographical draftsman deserve recognition.' The small plates of *Welsh Scenery*, however, are not especially interesting; they are accurate enough, no doubt, but lack liveliness.

An artist who became very much involved with portraying the scenery of Wales was Henry Gastineau, a drawing-master and watercolour painter who exhibited his work continuously for fifty-eight years. 'He excelled chiefly in landscapes chosen among wild and romantic scenery, rocks, cataracts, and rushing streams', commented Redgrave. The two volumes of his *Wales Illustrated*, published by Jones & Co at the Temple of the Muses, Finsbury Square, contain well over two hundred plates with the names of Wallis, Radclyffe, Varrall, Lacey, Adlard, Barber, Deeble and T. H. Shepherd among the many engravers (Plate 44). His total of 1,310 pictures shown at the galleries of the Old Water Colour Society is evidence of his industry. 'With his death,' wrote Martin Hardie, 'the old school of picturesque topography may be said to have expired.' He seems to have been virtually Wales's official artist, in succession to David Cox. Woodward's substantial *History of Wales, from the Earliest Times, To Its Final Incorporation With the Kingdom of England*, published in 1853, was illustrated by seventy-nine engravings after Gastineau, no other painter being represented. Nearly all the plates in Tillotson's *Picturesque Scenery in Wales* were also after his drawings, although Bartlett did manage to edge in towards the end of the volume.

An engraver particularly associated with Wales was William Radclyffe, who engraved all the plates, about a hundred, for Thomas Roscoe's *Wanderings and Excursions* in North and South Wales, first published 1836–7 and re-published in the 1850s. Most of the drawings for these volumes were by David Cox, an artist nearly as prolific as Gastineau, with a total of 973 works exhibited between 1805 and 1859, 849 of them at the Old Water Colour Society.

Plate 44 This view of Llanwrst Bridge after a drawing by Henry Gastineau was published in *Wales Illustrated*, 1830, and again in Woodward's *History of Wales*, 1853. The name of the engraver is not known

Cox taught painting, both at schools and privately; he also produced books of instruction, including *A Treatise on Landscape Painting and Effect in Water Colours*, 1814, and *The Young Artist's Companion*, 1825. The best of his work belongs with the best of watercolour painting, and some of the Welsh views which Radclyffe engraved are of very high quality. Other artists represented in Roscoe's volumes include Cox's son David, Copley Fielding, Cattermole, Creswick, E. Watson and H. Warren.

Thomas Roscoe's father, William, was a wealthy Liverpool merchant and a well-known patron of the arts. Thomas himself was one of the first travellers to mention using the railway; it seems likely that he also used the experience—and some of the words—of Benjamin Malkin, who had published his own excursions in South Wales at the beginning of the century. At times, the Roscoe style verges on the nauseating: 'Gentle readers', he says, 'would that ye could all behold the scenes to which my pleasant wanderings conducted me; would that ye could see them as I did, arrayed in their brightest and loveliest garb'. But he does provide some solid information to accompany

Radclyffe's well-executed plates. The engraver's ability to express so much in such small compass—five by three and a half inches—is remarkable; the views of Rhayadyr and the Vale of the Towy, both after David Cox, are good examples.

With improvements in the ferry service, the Isle of Wight became increasingly popular in the early 1800s as a tourist and holiday resort. It had already been the subject of two aquatint illustrated books published in the 1790s: Hassell's *Tour of the Isle of Wight*, with thirty plates, and Charles Tomkins' *Tour*, with seventy-eight sepia aquatints, some copies of which had the plates fully coloured. Gilpin had remarked on the island's picturesque beauties, and William Cooke had drawn and copper engraved several illustrations for *The New Picture of the Isle of Wight*, published in Southampton. Steam ferries and steel engraving arrived within a few years of each other, and a host of popular guidebooks began to appear. Among the better examples was *Barber's Picturesque Illustrations of the Isle of Wight*, with forty views, mostly drawn by Bartlett, engraved by T. Barber, Wallis, Winkles, Radclyffe, Tingle and Westwood, first published in 1835. The most popular and prolific of the island's illustrators, however, was George Brannon who, aided by members of his family, was artist, engraver and local publisher, issuing his own books from his publishing house at Wootton. What was probably his first work, *Vectis Scenery*, which he described as 'a series of original and select views, exhibiting the picturesque beauties, local peculiarities, and places of particular interest in the Isle of Wight', was a collection of etchings published in Southampton in 1825 and reissued several times from Wootton. A sequel to this, 'comprising such of the principal seats, or other views that are less frequently seen or visited', appeared in the 1820s. These were originally folio volumes, and comparatively costly; in later years Brannon reduced the size of his publications to quarto, octavo and duodecimo, to suit the pockets of the new and less wealthy visitors.

Many of Brannon's books ran to several editions, and a number of the plates appeared several times. Some of his titles, were almost essays in themselves: *Brannon's Graphic Delineations of the most prominent Objects in the Isle of Wight. Serving equally the Purposes of a useful Accompaniment to any of the un-illustrated local Guides, or as a Drawing-Book for copying in Pencil by the Tyro, and to assist the Amateur in Sketching from Nature.* Another was *Brannon's Picture of the Isle of Wight; or the expeditious Traveller's Index to its prominent Beauties & Objects of Interest. Compiled especially with Reference to those numerous visitors who can spare but two or three days to make the Tour of the Island.* The twenty engravings in the second title all appear to have been selected from the thirty engravings in the first, a nice example of what is today known as multipurpose use. His popular *Pleasure Visitor's Companion in Surveying the Isle of Wight*, a duodecimo volume first published in 1833, ran into five further editions in the next ten years.

One of the most renowned of the line engravers, working on both copper and steel, was John Le Keux; Britton wrote in a memoir, 'no English engraver has done more to enhance the fame of his art, and give peculiar interest and value to that branch which he professed and practised for so many years.' Le Keux, born in 1783, learnt the elements of engraving while working for his father, a pewterer by trade. From tankards he moved on to study under James Basire, where his attention was directed to architectural illustration. A few years later he was taken up by Britton, producing several hundred copper engravings for the *Beauties*, the *Architectural* and *Cathedral Antiquities* and similar publications.

John Le Keux is best known, however, for his steel engravings of Oxford and Cambridge. The *Memorials of Oxford* was published first as a periodical, fifty issues in all, between 1833 and 1837. The drawings were by F. Mackenzie and the text by the then President of Trinity, Dr Ingram; about two hundred wood engravings were contributed by one of the leading craftsmen of the time, Orlando Jewitt. The *Memorials* appeared in three volumes in 1837, published in Oxford and London. Some of the plates were used later in guide books issued by the Oxford publisher, J. H. Parker. Le Keux then turned to Cambridge, and serial publication of the *Memorials of Cambridge* was completed with the text by Thomas Wright and the Revd H. Longueville Jones, again accompanied by wood engravings. Mackenzie and J. A. Bell supplied the drawings. This project comprised thirty-eight numbers containing seventy-six plates. During the work Le Keux was frequently ill, but he had undertaken the publication at his own risk and pressed on to the end. According to Britton, 'the jealousy of local booksellers, and other annoyances incidental to the mode of publication which he had adopted, it is believed, caused him to regret his determination; but he persevered until the whole was finished.' The *Memorials* were later collected into two volumes. This was Le Keux's last major work; he died in 1844. His younger brother, Henry, was also a fine engraver, particularly noted for his vignettes after Turner for Samuel Rogers' *Poems*. His son, J. H. Le Keux, described as 'an honour to his parent and to his profession', kept up the tradition. The Le Keux family brought steel engraving of architectural subjects to the highest degree of perfection.

With greater mobility, resulting from the rapid growth of the railway network, the custom of taking holidays became much more widespread and the demand for cheap guidebooks increased. Steel engraving was one of the chief modes of illustration in the middle decades of the nineteenth century and among the leading publishers in this field was the Edinburgh firm of Adam and Charles Black. 'Without the pretensions of a tutor, dictating what he shall admire, the traveler will find these books very pleasing, intelligent, and instructive companions, giving him the exact knowledge he requires at the exact time he needs it', said a contemporary review of their publications. The volumes in the main series were not cheap: the third edition of *England & Wales* cost 10s 6d; the tenth edition of *Scotland* was 8s 6d, and the *English Lakes*, sixth edition, was 5s. But Black's also produced cheap editions, covering smaller areas, at one shilling each; Harriet Martineau's *Guide to Windermere*, with engravings by W. J. Linton after drawings by T. L. Apsland, could be bought in various formats at prices ranging from one shilling to a handsome demy quarto costing ten times as much. New editions of guides to some of the more popular areas appeared almost every year between 1840 and 1880, with illustrations by some of the most notable artists and engravers of the time.

It is worth studying one volume in rather more detail. The eleventh edition of Black's *Picturesque Tourist of Scotland* was published in 1854, having 'undergone a thorough revision and correction, the information, in several instances, having been either tested or re-written, from notes taken during tours recently made expressly for this work.' It contained over six hundred pages, with twenty-six maps, plans and railway charts and sixty-three illustrations, fifteen of them on steel and the others on wood. The engravings were by Miller, William Forrest, W. R. Smith, G. Aikman and William Chapman; the frontispiece, showing the entrance to Loch Scavaig from a painting by John Thomson, is a good example of Miller's work, and Forrest engraved a lively view of Glasgow Bridge after a drawing by A. Maclure. Indeed, all the steel engravings in this book are works of quality and character, and the same can be said of most of the wood engravings too. Bound in with the guide is 'Black's Guide Book Advertiser'; in this edition, a bookseller, Stephen Soulby of Ulverston, paid £4 3s to advertise 'books illustrative of Scottish Character and Scenery', including *Tourist's Memorial of Scotland*, with twenty views in fancy binding for five shillings, *Fingal's Cave*, two views drawn with the Camera Lucida by Thomas Allan, sixpence each, and *Annales Furnesienses*, by J. A. Beck, 'with 26 Steel Engravings by Le Keux, Wilmor, Carter &c; also Woodcuts, coloured Fac-similes, &c', originally published for seven guineas in a limited edition of two hundred and fifty copies and now reduced to £3 13s 6d, including postage. Bearing in mind these prices, it is interesting to note from the advertising section that bed and breakfast at the Albion

Temperance Hotel in Edinburgh cost three shillings and servants could be hired for one shilling a day.

Woodcuts, as they were cheaper to produce and could be printed easily with letterpress, provided the majority of guidebook illustrations until photography took over. Generally speaking, the higher the proportion of steel engravings a guidebook contained, the more expensive it was likely to be. The engravings themselves might appear several times in different publications, the plates having been sold off by one publisher and bought by another. Occasionally a really sumptuous edition appeared; the fifteenth edition of Black's *Picturesque Guide to the English Lakes*, with additional engravings by Edmund Evans after paintings by Myles Birket Foster, and a specially designed binding, is a noted example. The better Victorian publications, like those of Black and John Murray, make their modern equivalents with their vivid colour photographs look tawdry by comparison; however, we must remember that a good mid-nineteenth-century guidebook cost the equivalent of a day's full board and lodging in a respectable hotel, while today's version costs little more than a couple of fancy ice-creams and a bar of chocolate.

The early Victorian age also saw a rapid growth in the popularity of the small steel-engraved vignette. These were sometimes used in guidebooks; they also appeared without text in booklet collections or singly as embellishments to notepaper. One firm which specialised in these was the London-based publishers Rock & Co, who are said to have issued some seven thousand views in less than thirty years (Plate 45). The views covered the whole of the country, and nearly all of them are anonymous. Examples include *Views of Matlock & Derbyshire*, with fifty vignettes, *Views of the Isle of Wight* (one hundred), *24 Views and Scenery of Budleigh Salterton & Neighbourhood*, *Six Views of this Neighbourhood* (St Albans), and *80 Views of Harrogate & Neighbourhood*. They were issued until the mid 1870s and can be regarded as the Victorian equivalent to the picture postcard.

Several other firms issued similar sets of views, although none on such a large scale as Rock & Co. One of the earliest was J. & F. Harwood, who published three series, each containing forty-nine vignettes, under the title *Scenery of Great Britain*, 1841–2. Newman & Co was another London firm producing county collections of views, under the general title *Illustrations of British Scenery*. Vignettes were issued by local publishers as well. Henry Besley of Exeter published some 'Illustrations of Devon', beginning in 1848 with a set of engravings after drawings by George Townsend, a local artist. In the 1860s Besley brought out various bound collections of prints, including *Views in Cornwall* (twenty-four), and *Views of Devonshire*, totalling sixty-six vig-

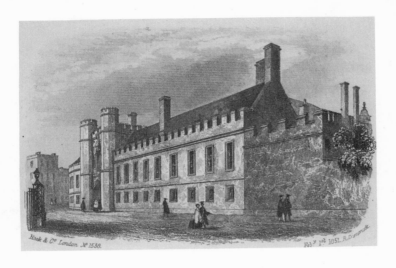

Plate 45 Christ's College, Cambridge. This vignette is number 1538 of Rock & Company's designs and is shown here as used on writing paper. It was first issued in 1851

nettes. These prints also appeared bound together in small sets each covering a particular area. In Kent, H. Barley published *Thirty Views of Ramsgate*, and J. Bourner produced twelve vignette *Views of Dover. Thirty Views of Hastings and St Leonards* were brought out by a Hastings firm, Thorpe, about 1870. These are just a few examples of local enterprise; research in local record offices and libraries will produce very many more. Bound sets of these vignette views are not easy to find nowadays but there are plenty of single specimens around. Victorian scrapbooks usually contain them, sometimes simply removed from their binding and sometimes cut from the notepaper on which occasionally they appeared. Besley's early vignettes were sold on letter paper for two-pence each, but cost sixpence on drawing paper.

These vignettes bring the story of topographical line engraving on copper or steel virtually to a close. They may be of little artistic merit but they have their value as pictorial records of the landscapes and townscapes of their time. The last decades of the nineteenth century saw a few new editions of books first published earlier; there was a Finden's *Ports and Harbours* in 1874, and a new edition of Browne's *History of the Highlands and of the Highland Clans*, with about thirty topographical views among the sixty-six engravings, appeared in the following year. As late as 1890, W. Banks & Co issued a set of twenty-five anonymous plates under the title *Scenery in the Western Highlands on the Route from Oban to Iona, Staffa and Glencoe*. But the engravers' own society, the

Chalcographic Society, had disbanded many years before. Founded about 1810 for the leading engravers to meet and discuss new ideas and techniques it had been in existence for some fifty years. And in 1901, Alfred Whitman, of the Prints and Drawings Department of the British Museum, wrote in the first edition of *The Print Collector's Handbook* that 'line engraving has declined, until at the present day scarcely a member of the fraternity survives'. The great William Miller had died in 1882, at the age of eighty-six, and J. C. Armytage, who had successfully re-engraved many plates after Turner, died in 1897.

Some Victorian line-engraved topography found a last resting-place in the warehouses of jobbing printers. The Bristol firm of E. S. and A. Robinson employed at one time fifteen engravers (and nine 'artistic lithographic' drawers) to produce illustrations for their products, mostly paper bags. Their stock book showed examples of over three hundred topographical views from which customers could make their selection. These views do not show much originality, some of them being copied from photographs or woodcuts from periodicals such as the *Illustrated London News*. They can still sometimes be found in Victorian scrapbooks for, crude though most of the views were, they had some appeal for the collector.

5

WOOD CUTTING AND ENGRAVING

In the history of English reproductive art, no method has been more dominated by the achievement of a single person than the art of wood engraving: Thomas Bewick, born in 1753, was a giant in his field. In topographical illustration during the eighteenth and nineteenth centuries, reproductions from wood blocks are not of major importance, being confined almost entirely to books and periodicals, but because these books and periodicals had, in many instances, a wide circulation, it would be wrong to omit them from our study or to underrate their influence. However, apart from the work of Bewick and some of his pupils, most of the products have little artistic merit.

Wood cutting was a popular craft of the fifteenth and sixteenth centuries, and the cuts after Dürer and Holbein were enormously popular. Because the lines used for printing from wood stand up in relief, wood blocks can be printed on the same press as type; this was therefore the simplest method for book illustration as well as the cheapest. Wood blocks were used to illustrate devotional works and chapbooks, but were ignored by the growing print trade of the eighteenth century which concentrated on line engraving on copper. The work on wood was generally clumsily executed and poorly printed, until Bewick took the old craft and made it into an art in which the English achievement can rank with the best.

In 1767, then aged fourteen, Bewick was apprenticed to Ralph Beilby, an engraver of Newcastle upon Tyne. In his *Memoir* he described the business he had joined:

> Such was the industry of my master that he refused nothing, coarse or fine—he under took every thing & did it in the best way he could—he fitted up & tempered his own tools, which he adapted to every purpose

& learned me to do the same—this readiness to undertake, brought him in an overflow of work & our work place was filled with the coarsest kind of steel stamps—pipe Moulds—Bottle moulds—Brass Clock faces —Door plates—Coffin plates—Bookbinders Letters & stamps—Steel, Silver & gold Seals—Mourning Rings—Arms crests & cyphers on silver & every kind of job, from the Silver Smiths—writing engraving of Bills, bank notes, Bills of parcels, shop bills & cards . . . but what he most excelled in was ornamental Silver engraving: in this, as far as I am able to judge he was one of the first in the Kingdom— & I think upon the whole, he might be called 'an ingeneous self taught Artist'.

One aspect of the work, however, 'the higher department of engraving such as Landscape or historical plates', Beilby had not attempted before Bewick joined the firm. Later he went to London to take lessons, but there was little call in Newcastle for plates of this kind and Beilby had few opportunities of practising his new-found skill.

Beilby himself neither enjoyed engraving on wood nor was good at it. When work of this kind was required he handed it over to Bewick who between 1771 and 1779 produced a large number of blocks for books, printed in Newcastle by Thomas Saint, including *Youth's Instructive and Entertaining Storyteller*, *Select Fables* and *Fables by the late Mr Gay*. Beilby was so impressed by the results that he sent impressions of some of the *Fables* blocks to the Society for the Encouragement of the Arts, who awarded Bewick a premium of seven guineas. During this period Bewick had completed his apprenticeship and had spent a few months in London, intending to seek a living there. 'I did not like London', he wrote; 'it appeared to me to be a World of itself where every thing in the extreme, might at once be seen—extreme riches—extreme poverty—extreme Grandeur & extreme wretchedness—all of which were such as I had not contemplated upon before . . . I tired of it & determind to return home—The Country of my old friends—the manners of the people of that day—the scenery of Tyne side, seemed altogether to form a paradise for me & I longed to see it again.' Soon after his return to Newcastle he entered in-to partnership with Ralph Beilby and they worked together for the next twenty years.

Bewick did not invent a new method of wood engraving. What he did was to use the tools of the metal engraver, and something of the technique, on sections of boxwood cut across the grain. It seems to have been Dr Charles Hutton, author of a *Treatise on Mensuration*, who first showed Bewick and Beilby how to do this when he approached them to produce the diagrams for his book. This method had already been in use for about a hundred years but had not been seen in Newcastle where—as in most other places—wood blocks for illustration were customarily made by cutting out along the grain with a chisel or a knife. Bewick saw the surface of the block as black and the lines he made as white. To start with, he would make a watercolour painting or a drawing of his subject. According to Iain Bain, in his introduction to Bewick's *Memoir*:

> these were then heavily leaded on the back with soft pencil, after which the paper was placed over the selected piece of boxwood and the edges folded over to steady the position . . . A fine hard point was then used to trace the basic outlines of the designs. Under the pressure these were transferred to the surface of the block which had previously been prepared with brick dust so that it would pick up the pencil carbon more readily.

Bain quotes John Dovaston, who wrote an account of Bewick's life for the *Magazine of Natural History* in 1829, as saying that Bewick did not usually draw much detail on the block but added it with the burin directly.

It is, of course, for his birds, his animals, and his 'tail-pieces' that Bewick is best known. His landscapes are usually incidental, the background to the portrait of a living creature or to an incident that makes a moral point. Some of the best are tail-pieces to the two volumes of *British Birds*, almost anticipating the steel-engraved vignettes after Turner in the way they grow out of the white paper around them (Plate 46). In his *Hand-Book for Young Painters*, C. R. Leslie wrote:

> The student of Landscape can never consult the works of Bewick without improvement. The backgrounds to his figures of his Quadrupeds and Birds, and his vignettes, have a charm of Nature quite his own. He gives us, in these, every season of the year; and his trees, whether in the clothing of summer, or in the nakedness of winter, are the trees of an artist bred in the country. He is equally true in his little home scenes, his farm-yards and cottages, as in his wild coast scenery, with flocks of sea-birds wheeling round the rocks . . . .

It seems an instinctive vision, undisturbed by picturesque theory and influenced by no one. Sometimes, however, there is an Aesop-like moral: for example, the well-known tail-piece showing a farmer driving his cow across a river to avoid paying the toll for using the nearby bridge, while his hat, costing far more than the toll, floats away on the stream. William Ivins described

Plate 46 'The Ruined Cottage', engraved on wood by Thomas Bewick and Luke Clennell. It appeared as a tail-piece in the 1847 edition of *British Birds*, Volume II

Bewick's tail-pieces as having a 'salty, rural sentimentality'; they also show a keen eye for detail and deep personal knowledge of the countryside, mostly of south Northumberland and north Durham which were within walking distance of Bewick's home territory of Eltringham and Ovingham on the Tyne, a few miles west of Newcastle.

A number of apprentices learnt their craft under Bewick when he set up his own workshop in St Nicholas's churchyard. Not all were wood engravers—throughout his life Bewick continued to work largely on metal—but several of them cut wood blocks from their master's designs and, as they grew more proficient, from their own. Bewick regretted the time he wasted on 'useless and wicked pupils', but many of his apprentices he spoke of with affection and praise. The first was his brother John who, after many vicissitudes, eventually settled down to wood engraving for the London publisher William Bulmer, but who died aged thirty-five before his promise was fully realised. Others included Charlton Nesbit, who worked in Newcastle and London, where he made wood engravings for some of Ackermann's publications; Henry Hole, who did some designs for Ackermann's *Religious Emblems*; John Anderson, engraver of the blocks for Bloomfield's *The Farmer's Boy*, 1800; Edward Willis, noted for his good behaviour; John Harrison, Bewick's nephew, expert in the engraving of writing on metal; and Henry White, who went to London after completing his apprenticeship, ' & chiefly turned his attention to the imitation of sketchy cross hatching on Wood, from the inimitable pencil of Mr Cruikshanks', later illustrating several books.

There were four particularly distinguished pupils. Luke Clennell was apprenticed from 1797 to 1804. He cut some of the tail-pieces for the second volume of *British Birds* and his name appears with Bewick's on the title-page of

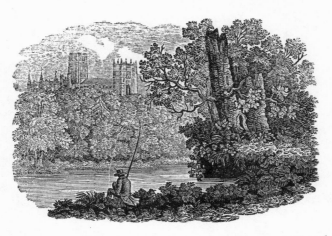

Plate 47 'The Fisherman at Durham'. This block was probably engraved by Thomas Bewick but may be the work of Isaac Nicholson. It was not published until 1870

The Hive of Ancient and Modern Literature, collected and published by A. Hodgson of Newcastle. After moving to London he worked on many other books, his woodcuts after Stothard sharing the illustration of Rogers' *Pleasure of Memory* with the steel engravings of Turner's vignettes. Nearly all of Greig's engravings for Sir Walter Scott's *Border Antiquities* are after paintings by Clennell, who had developed into a very fine watercolourist. In 1817, aged thirty-six, he went mad and never regained his reason, dying in 1840. Isaac Nicholson set up his own engraving business in Newcastle where he produced an annual called *The Fisher's Garland* (Plate 47). William Harvey, 'one of the first in excellence', completed his apprenticeship in 1817 and went on to London where he became famous as a designer for wood blocks, providing the illustrations for many books published between 1820 and 1840. Robert, Thomas Bewick's son, eventually became a partner in the firm and after his father's death in 1828 took over until he himself died twenty-one years later. Another apprentice, John Jackson, not mentioned by Bewick in his *Memoir*, became an authority on the craft and co-author of *A Treatise on Wood Engraving*, 1839. It was Jackson who made the well-known engraving of Bewick's premises by the churchyard, with its sign over the window 'Bewick & Son, Engravers and Copperplate Printers'. To distinguish between the work of Bewick and his apprentices is not always possible, but whatever came out of the workshop must have had the master's approval.

Bewick and his pupils gave a new direction to book illustration, but there was a contemporary of Bewick's who should not be forgotten. This was John

Thurston, born in Scarborough in 1774, who began his career as a copperplate engraver, working for James Heath, but later turned to wood. Bewick knew Thurston, who had in fact been brought up on the outskirts of Newcastle, and described him as 'ingenious'. Thurston was a designer rather than an engraver; he drew directly on to the wood which was then cut by a trained craftsman. One such craftsman was Charlton Nesbit, who Bewick said was the first to do justice to Thurston's designs. Thurston designed for many publications, including Ackermann's *Religious Emblems*, an edition of Shakespeare, and Somerville's *Rural Sports*; he also worked for the Chiswick Press, and had a strong influence on Victorian wood engraving.

Wood engraving was extensively used in magazines and periodicals in the nineteenth century. Leading the field was the *Illustrated London News*, founded in 1843, with *The Graphic* its nearest rival. The large pictures in these periodicals were composed of several blocks; these were clamped together for the sketch to be drawn over the whole surface, then taken apart and distributed to several engravers each of whom worked to cut his section of the sketch on to his block. This completed, the blocks were again locked together for a master engraver to complete the joins and finish the design. The whole thing was then printed, possibly over a double page. If you look carefully at a copy of one of these periodicals, you can sometimes detect where the small blocks joined. The method was quick, economical and reasonably efficient, and a larger number of copies could be run without any visible deterioration. A vast multitude of rather dreary pictures was produced in this way. It is interesting to note that single pages from these Victorian periodicals are now appearing for sale— mounted and hand-coloured —as good steel engravings become rarer and hence more expensive.

Topographical wood engraving is chiefly to be found in nineteenth-century guidebooks. Two artists stand out. One was George Bonner, born in Devizes in 1796 and trained as a wood engraver in London. Among the guides he illustrated were *The Picturesque Pocket Companion to Margate, Ramsgate, Broadstairs, and the Parts Adjacent*, first published 1831, *Kidd's New Guide to the 'Lions' of London*, 1832, and *Picturesque Excursions; containing upwards of four hundred views at and near places of popular resort*, by Arthur Freeling, 1839. Bonner also engraved for the *British Cyclopaedia*, and his work is well above the average for its time in its skilful handling of gradation of tone. Some of his blocks were used for other publications, many years after his death, in 1836, but they needed good printing and paper—as with all quality wood engraving—to do them justice. The Chiswick Press, which printed the *Pocket Companion* and *Kidd's New Guide*, provided these, but other printers of guidebooks seldom did so.

A wood engraver with an even higher reputation was Orlando Jewitt, whose first illustrations were published before he reached his sixteenth birthday. Architecture, antiquities and natural history were his principal interests. He made the wood engravings for Ingram's *Memorials of Oxford* to accompany the fine steel engravings of John Le Keux; Jewitt's blocks were used again in J. H. Parker's *Hand-Book for Visitors to Oxford*, 1847. Among the very many other books in which his engravings appeared were Murray's *Cathedrals*, the *Archaeological Journal*, Scott's *Westminster Abbey*, and various editions of a number of guidebooks to York, Scarborough, Ripon, Alderley Edge and the Lakes. He also engraved for several volumes on natural history, and in all is one of the most notable and prolific illustrators of the mid-nineteenth century.

As photography edged in, the wood engravers fought hard to retain their livelihood. There is a great deal of attractive work to be found in the books and magazines of the second half of the century. Mr and Mrs S. C. Hall's *Book of the Thames* and *Book of South Wales, the Wye and the Coast*, both reprinted from the *Art Journal*, contain some pleasant cuts. Many of those in the *Thames* were after drawings by W. S. Coleman and were executed by a variety of engravers including the well-known Dalziel brothers and the firm of Butterworth & Heath. The clear and informative plates in H. R. Robertson's *Life on the Upper Thames*, 1875, were engraved by W. J. Palmer after the author's own drawings. The travel books published by the Religious Tract Society were lavishly illustrated by wood engravings, some of good quality; again the name of Butterworth & Heath recurs, among a great deal of anonymous work. A periodical which appeared later in the century, Cassell's *Rivers of Great Britain*, contained a mixture of photographs and wood engravings, with pride of place being given to the 'Rembrandt Photogravure Plates' printed in sepia and of considerable quality.

As an art form wood engraving still continues. But much research still needs to be done on the workshop craftsmen of the nineteenth century, whose products as they grow in age will surely come to be more highly valued.

6

ETCHING

Compared to line engraving, etching was little used for topographical illustration in Britain during the period we are examining (Plate 48). A few of the major painters—Gainsborough and Cotman are two examples—etched some plates themselves, and a few lesser artists also tried their hands. But for the most part etching was used as the groundwork for line engraving or aquatint; the etcher's needle drew the skeleton of the composition, to which the details, light and shade were later added by one of the other methods. As we have seen, this was the way in which many of the greatest engravings were produced; those after Turner, for instance, when Turner himself often made the etching, and those by F. C. Lewis, who executed all the work himself.

The seventeenth-century topographical etchings by Wenceslaus Hollar had little immediate influence, although in a sense they showed others the possibilities of the medium. Two of the first of our native-born etchers were Francis Barlow and Francis Place. Barlow's best work portrayed animals and birds, but Place, who also used mezzotint, produced some fine landscape work, less formal and more atmospheric than Hollar's. His 'On the Ouse at York' is a good specimen of his achievement, and several of his marine pieces are also of high quality. Place died in 1728, having made most of his etchings early in his career, and for many decades no Englishman of comparable ability took up the craft. The first half of the eighteenth century saw a growing interest in Rembrandt's etchings—and an outcrop of forgeries—but it was not until the time of Gainsborough and Paul Sandby that any significant work was done, at least in landscape.

Paul Sandby's first etchings were made when he was seventeen, most of his

Plate 48 (*opposite*) A self-explanatory etching by George Cruikshank, 1859

'O'- I've seen Etching' it's easy enough, you only rub some black stuff over the Copper plate, & then take a etching needle, & scratch away a bit — & then clap on some d—ke—ta—ke — and there you are !

A Journeyman printer's description of the art of Etching on Copper.

Etched by George Cruikshank when describing the process of Etching at a Hampstead Conversazione on the 4th of May — 1859

First proof —   Geo Cruikshank

early scenes being of Scottish landscapes and castles. He completed at least a hundred plates—for that was the number on sale in 1765 for £1 7s from two London dealers. It states on some of his views that they were made on the spot, which one can well believe from their liveliness and accuracy of detail. Etching was also used with engraving in contributions to his brother Thomas's *Views of Windsor Great Park* showing the landscaping work in progress under Thomas's supervision as deputy ranger.

Gainsborough had what was for his time an unfashionably high opinion of landscape painting, and of Paul Sandby, whom he described as 'the only Man of Genius . . . who has employ'd his Pencil that way'. For himself he once wrote that he was tired of Portraits 'and wish very much to take my Viol da Gamba and walk off to some sweet village where I can paint Landskips and enjoy the fag End of Life in quietness and ease.' He was always ready to investigate new ideas and developments, and different ways of looking at things; he made a study of 'a Man sketching using a Claude glass' and was fascinated by the Eidophusikon of de Loutherbourg. His own 'showbox' survives in the Victoria and Albert Museum. Through a lens in this box you could view landscapes which he had painted on sheets of glass and which were lit from the back by candles. Gainsborough was quick to experiment with newly introduced methods which imitated the effects of painting and drawing and he produced several aquatints and soft-ground etchings during the 1770s. The subjects of his etchings were perhaps idealised; his 'Gypsies' of the early 1750s are an element in a careful composition—picturesque gypsies, in fact. They are part of the Gainsborough dream; he may have wished to walk off to some sweet village, but most of his landscapes were composed from models which he built up in the studio from various odds and ends.

Much late eighteenth-century etching was an attempt to reproduce cheaply the drawings and paintings of the old masters. Gainsborough's own work was treated in this way by John Laporte and William Frederick Wells, both known as watercolour painters, who between them produced seventy-two soft-ground etchings after sketches by Gainsborough between 1801 and 1804. Of these, Laporte made thirty-three; he had also previously published a set of etchings, *Studies of Trees*, as well as plates of mainly Welsh topographical views. But, leaving aside this type of work, the most interesting and influential etching of this period can be found in the political and satirical work of Hogarth, Rowlandson and Gillray, outside the limits of our present study.

It was the Norwich artists of the early nineteenth century who succeeded in establishing a strong tradition in landscape etching in this country. Before we turn to them, however, let us look at one or two others who produced work of quality and should not be ignored. There was George Smith of Chichester, whose landscape paintings, according to Samuel Redgrave, 'were pleasing ... but mere imitations of Claude and Poussin. In his day they were lauded beyond their merits, fashion placed him in the front rank, poets apostrophised him, and the Society of Arts awarded him in 1760 their first premium in competition with Richard Wilson.' His brother John helped him in the production of fifty-three etched plates, with some engraving, of pretty pastoral Sussex scenes (Plate 49), mostly imaginary. John Clerk of Eldin made several etchings of Scottish landscapes and buildings between 1777 and 1779. In addition to his lithographs, Thomas Barker of Bath etched several romantic landscapes, and Sawrey Gilpin, brother of the 'picturesque' William, etched animal subjects. The *Antiquities of York*, 1813, were etched by Henry Cave on forty folio plates; the *Antiquities of Suffolk*, etched by Henry Davey, appeared a few years later, followed in 1820 by his *Views of Bury St Edmunds*. Etchings of cathedrals were made by J. C. Buckler, 1822, and by John Coney, whose plates were especially notable for their vast size. Sound architectural etching was also produced by the brothers Daniel and Samuel Lysons, particularly for their *Magna Britannia*, published in six volumes between 1806 and 1822, a thorough and well-illustrated topographical account of the counties of Great Britain in alphabetical order which, unfortunately, only got as far as Devonshire.

One of the finest of the books of this time illustrated by etchings was *The Principal Rivers of Wales* by John George Wood, published by T. Bensley in London in 1813. This contained 157 plates, delicately tinted and worked, of which twenty-four are double page. William Daniell did his own etching for the 308 plates of the *Voyage around Great Britain* before they went off to be aquatinted. Another etcher of high quality was George Cuitt, who produced three sets of etchings of Chester, a series of views of Yorkshire abbeys and seventy-five scenes in Wales. His works were collected by the publisher Nattali and appeared in 1848 under the title *Wanderings and Pencillings amongst the Ruins of Olden Time*. The engraver Robert Brandard also issued a set of etchings in the 1840s, under the title *Scraps of Nature*; again, this was work of good quality. Of lesser merit was the work of David Charles Read, who published three collections totalling over 150 plates, *Wiltshire Scenery*, 1831, *Lake Scenery*, 1840, and *Etchings from Nature*, 1845.

While no other locality produced a 'school' of etching to rival Norwich, the West Country did attract a few able exponents. Thomas Hewitt Williams,

Plate 49 (*overleaf*) Cottage in Sussex, etched by G. and J. Smith

Drawn & etch'd by Robt Dixon

a landscape painter also known later as a lithographer, had his *Picturesque Excursions in Devonshire and Cornwall*, consisting of three parts, previously issued separately, with twenty etchings accompanying a well-written text, published by Murray & Harding in 1804. He seems to have journeyed on foot, and he followed these expeditions with *The Environs of Exeter*, 1815–16, with six etchings in the first part and five engravings by others after his own drawings in the second. The Plymouth-born artist Samuel Prout, whom we have met as one of the many artists employed by Britton and Brayley on the *Beauties*, completed about two hundred soft-ground etchings. Some of them were published by Thomas Palser in 1812, under the title *Picturesque Delineations in the Counties of Devon and Cornwall*; others were published by Ackermann: *Studies of Cottages and Rural Scenery Drawn and Etched in Imitation of Chalk*, 1816, and *Samuel Prout's New Drawing Book in the Manner of Chalk*, containing twelve picturesque cottages in Devon and Somerset. Another Plymouth artist, William Payne, brought out a set of *Six Views near Plymouth*; in or about 1810. And Frederic Christian Lewis, although not born in the West Country, found there the subjects for much of his landscape work. For his *Scenery of the River Dart*, 1821, he made both the etchings and aquatints, nearly all of them after his own originals. *The Scenery of the Rivers Tamar and Tavy*, published two years later, consisted entirely of etchings, forty-seven in all, and this was followed in 1827 by *The Scenery of the River Exe*, with thirty-four etchings, confident and showing a sure professional touch.

The Norwich Society was founded in 1803. In recent years it has been regarded as the focus of English provincial painting, but in its time Norwich was no more generous to its artists than any other English provincial city. John Crome was unable to make a living by selling his pictures; he had to teach as well, and it was still a struggle. Between 1809 and 1814 he etched thirty-four plates, nine of them in soft ground. In most of them trees are the principal subject, trees standing by water or at the side of a country road, their branches interlacing with the sky. They pointed the direction for Crome's later oil paintings such as 'Marlingford Grove', 'Poringland Oak', 'Bury Road Scene', and 'Wood Scene with a Pool'. The etching of one of his favourite subjects, 'Mousehold Heath by Norwich', was treated with strength and a sense of visual excitement. None of these etchings was published in Crome's lifetime, possibly because Dawson Turner, the Norfolk banker who was a patron of Crome and other Norwich artists, did not think they were sufficiently finished to gain a good reception. After Crome's death, thirty-one of the plates were published by his widow, under the title *Norfolk Picturesque Scenery*, 1834, sixty sets being printed. They were slow to sell, and Dawson Turner seems to have proposed tidying up and 'improving' the plates for reissue, with a Memoir by himself. Henry Ninham and W. C. Edwards were given the task of altering the plates. One of the alterations entailed removing the dramatic sky of 'Mousehold Heath' and replacing it with the parallel ruled lines of the engraver. This was not the only sky thus treated; Ninham, a painter himself and an etcher of quality, rejected the accusations that he was responsible for the alteration and it may have been the engraver Edwards of Bungay who defaced Crome's plates, possibly at the insistence of John Berney Crome and Dawson Turner. The soft-ground etchings, of which eight were published, were not tampered with. They are among the finest examples of this method ever produced in England.

Among other Norwich artists who began etching about the same time as Crome were Robert Dixon and John Sell Cotman. Dixon, born in 1780, studied at the Royal Academy and became for a time a scene painter for the Norwich theatre, before taking up that typically Norwich profession of drawing-master. His thirty-eight collected etchings, all in soft ground, were published in 1812 as *Picturesque Norfolk Scenery*, an appropriate title for these pleasantly composed rustic views of pretty cottages (Plate 50). Towards the end of his short life Dixon suffered much from ill-health; he died in 1815, leaving a widow and six children.

Etching was far more important to John Sell Cotman than it was to Crome. For Crome, etching seems to have been almost a private, contemplative activity, and it occupied him for only a few years. But for Cotman it was a major part of his artistic life and his total of etched plates was little short of four hundred. Despite his remarkable early watercolours and drawings, including the views of Rokeby and the Greta, Cotman had not succeeded in being elected a member of the Water Colour Society. He found difficulty in establishing himself as a teacher in Norwich, where he was in competition with Crome, and was forced to look in other directions for a source of income. Encouraged by Dawson Turner he took up etching, particularly of antiquities. His first collection, *Miscellaneous Etchings*, was published in 1811 and contained twenty-six plates, ranging from architectural studies—'The Old College House, Conway', is one of the finest with its closely studied variety of textures —to rural subjects, of which 'Trees in Duncombe Park' is a good example.

Cotman's next venture was *The Architectural Antiquities of Norfolk*, issued in parts from 1811 onwards and completed, sixty plates in all, in 1818. This was

Plate 50 (*overleaf*) Sketch at Pulham Market, a soft-ground etching by Robert Dixon from his *Picturesque Norfolk Scenery* collection. This plate was first published in 1810

no great financial success; some of the parts were issued late and some of the subscribers fell by the wayside. Best known of these plates are the views of the South Gate at Yarmouth and St Benet's Abbey, superb examples both of composition and of the art of etching. For the next few years Cotman continued with architectural work, frequently travelling to France to sketch for *The Architectural Antiquities of Normandy*, published in 1822. During this period he also etched some plates in soft ground. Henry Bohn bought the plates and published them in 1838 with the title *Liber Studiorum*, although Cotman himself had intended to produce a collection of mezzotints inspired by Turner's *Liber* under this title. According to Bohn, these etchings had been made 'more for practice and amusement' than for any other reason. They included some Welsh scenes deriving from Cotman's early sketching tours in the first years of the century as well as views of what the artist himself called 'rare and beautiful Norfolk'. Cotman's *Liber* contained forty-eight plates, of which thirty-nine were soft-ground etchings, and it is perhaps the most varied and interesting of all his published collections of prints.

Several more Norwich painters, some of whom had been Crome's pupils, tried their hands at etching, although none on anything like the scale of Cotman. Joseph Stannard was among the more successful, with a dozen or so landscapes, often with figures. James Stark and George Vincent were rather less effective with the etching needle than with oils or watercolours, but Thomas Lound produced some good waterside scenes using drypoint. John Middleton, some of whose watercolours must rank with the finest of the nineteenth century, also excelled in his few landscape etchings, delicate and carefully worked. More prolific was Henry Ninham, who produced four collections between 1840 and 1861: *Picturesque Antiquities*, *Views of Norwich and Norfolk*, *Gates of Norwich*, and *City Gates*, a total of sixty-nine plates altogether. Looking at the achievements of the Norwich etchers, it is difficult to follow the reasoning of P. G. Hamerton, who wrote in *The Graphic Arts*, 1882, that 'for a long time before the modern revival of etching, it was treated with a degree of contempt which is hardly imaginable now'.

But Hamerton's was a prejudiced view; as a champion of Seymour Haden, he had little praise for anyone who did not etch in a similar manner, and dismissed or ignored a large body of valuable work. A quite different attitude was expressed by Alfred Ashley, author of *The Art of Etching on Copper*, first published 1849. He referred to 'the increased and increasing attention now given to this beautiful branch of the Fine Arts', which had induced him to write his instructional manual. For whom his book was intended he quickly made clear.

For Ladies, this art is peculiarly adapted: the fact of Her Majesty making it a principal amusement, and, apart from her multifarious duties, evidently giving it so much of her time and attention, will, perhaps, be deemed sufficient proof of this assertion; but, if more be wanting, the mastery obtained over it by the female hand, is clearly exemplified in the beautiful etchings illustrating the Babes in the Wood, by the accomplished Marchioness of Waterford.

Ashley's was one of a large number of nineteenth-century instructional books, several of which, like George Brookshaw's *A New Treatise on Flower Painting*, with its sub-title 'or every lady her own drawing master', had what might today be described as an inbuilt sexist bias. Most of them dealt with water-colour painting and drawing, but John Hassell's *Graphic Delineations*, published in the 1820s, was devoted to the art of etching, 'or manner of copying pictures and drawings by a method at once scientific, tasteful and amusing', clearly an occupation for the amateur.

By no means amateur—or feminine—was the work of James Fittler, who early in the century made fifty etchings after John Claude Nattes for *Scotia Depicta*, described as 'powerful in light and shade, hard and not agreeable in manner', or the thirty *Rural Subjects* etched by William Delamotte, drawing-master to the Royal Military Academy at Great Marlow, published in 1816. Other male practitioners included Francis Stevens, who etched over fifty farmhouses and cottages for publication by Ackermann in 1815, and George Fennel Robson, 'a most persevering student', who came to London when only sixteen and succeeded in earning his living through drawing. He toured Scotland, making forty etchings of the Grampian Mountains, and submitted 653 paintings to the Old Water Colour Society in the space of nineteen years. The Scottish painter Andrew Geddes was also a skilful etcher, mainly in dry-point, producing a few good landscapes as well as a large number of plates after his own portraits. David Wilkie etched some plates as well, mostly in drypoint, but he was more concerned with selling the engraving rights for his own paintings, from which he made a great deal of money.

In 1838 the Etching Club was founded. During the mid-century decades its many members needled happily away, oblivious to the advances in the art that were happening in France, where the work of Charles Meryon, in partic-ular, was adding a new dimension to etching. The brothers Richard and Samuel Redgrave were in succession secretaries to the Club, Samuel—compiler of the useful *Dictionary of Artists of the English School*—holding the office from 1842 until his death in 1874. Among other leading members were the Academicians Thomas Creswick and Charles West Cope, as well as a number of worthy ladies. In 1850, Samuel Palmer—arguably the Club's greatest member—joined. Now aged forty-five Palmer had already completed his finest work in oil and watercolour. In the years between 1850 and 1881, when he died, he made thirteen etchings and left four more unfinished. In the best of these works he recaptured the almost mystical vision of his earlier years at Shoreham, but it was a vision which he had to work at day after day to express. Unlike the freely drawn plates of Seymour Haden and Whistler, with their large areas of white space, Palmer's designs seem to emerge gradually from the dark, yielding more and more to the observer the longer he studies them.

Opinions vary as to the value of Palmer's etched studies. Arthur M. Hind said that as an etcher of landscape he was 'an artist of no great power', while P. G. Hamerton felt that his work was over-finished. In contrast is the comment by Richard Godfrey that the 'Sleeping Shepherd; Early Morning' is 'an etching that by itself would have justified the Club's existence'; and Leslie Parris of the Tate Gallery considered his etchings 'among the best of his later works'. The two plates that perhaps make the greatest impact are 'The Bellman' and 'The Lonely Tower', both dating from 1879. They are not portraits of landscape but visions, which can be felt as well as seen, the gleams of light ('make friends of the white paper' Palmer said) seeming to shine out from the graduated blackness of the composition.

English etching became 'respectable' both socially and artistically in 1880, with the foundation of the Royal Society of Painter-Etchers and Engravers whose first president was Seymour Haden. Whistler, Sickert, Strang and Short took the art into the twentieth century. For many critics they brought a higher degree of professional achievement than had been seen in England before. Hind described Whistler—born in America but living mostly in London—as 'the greatest personality in the history of modern etching' and gives highest praise to two early twentieth-century etchers, David Cameron and Muirhead Bone, which takes us outside the period of this present study. But the achievements of some of their predecessors have not always been given their full credit. This may in part be due to the assumption that most etching before the so-called 'etching revival' of the later nineteenth century consisted merely in copying someone else's drawing on to a copper plate. We have seen that this was not so, and in conclusion can refer to three artists, not so far mentioned, whose work in different ways was outstanding during the period.

First of these three is the amateur of the Norwich School, the Revd E. T. Daniell, at one time a pupil of Crome, who made several fine landscape etchings between 1824 and 1835. A quick and sensitive sketcher—he exhibited

Plate 51 A fine example of the etched work of Edward William Cooke, showing a herring-boat unloading at Yarmouth Quay. This plate was first published in 1829 and was included in Cooke's collection *Shipping and Craft*

a handful of paintings at the Academy and the Royal Institute—he was able to use the etching needle with equal facility, and his work won the respect of many painters of his day, including Turner. Then there was Edward William Cooke, son of the engraver George and nephew of William Bernard; etching and engraving were family pursuits. Better known as a marine and coastal painter, Edward Cooke published in 1831 a splendid collection of sixty-five etchings of shipping, notable for their close attention to detail (Plate 51). And finally, the man best known as a *Punch* illustrator, Charles Samuel Keene. Keene drew and etched exactly what he saw. Several of his thirty-four plates are landscapes, or rather 'beach scapes', scenes of the Suffolk coast, including Southwold and his favourite Dunwich. 'England has Keene, he does not exhibit, he is not fashionable, and that is everything', wrote the elder Pissarro. Unlike some of the 'etching revival' heavyweights, Keene did not lay down the law on either art or life and emphasised only the importance of working from nature. If an artist can be described as characteristically English, then that description is appropriate to no one more than to Charles Keene.

7

METHODS

There is no shortage of instructional material on the various methods of reproduction that we have discussed. In this Guide, however, the subject is examined historically, and it seems appropriate to look at the methods and the way they were used at the time when the prints we are considering were being produced. Theodore Henry Adolphus Fielding was the eldest son of a portrait painter, Theodore Nathan, and the brother of Anthony Vandyke Copley, distinguished as a watercolour painter and president of the Old Water Colour Society, of Thales, watercolourist and teacher of drawing, and of Newton, watercolourist, engraver and lithographer. Theodore Henry specialised in landscape drawing and engraving; he was also a teacher of drawing and perspective and published several instructional books. One of them was *The Art of Engraving*, published by Ackermann & Co in 1841. It is from this book that the following chapter has been extracted; no alterations have been made, although some paragraphs not relevant to our survey have been omitted.

ETCHING

We shall consider etching, not as the beginning of line engraving, or as practised by line engravers, but as generally executed by painters. In this style the needle and aquafortis are the only means employed, the graver being seldom called into action, and the parallel ruler for ruling flat tints, *never*.

The process of etching consists in covering a metal plate with a varnish called etching-ground, through which the lines composing the subject are drawn with a sharp-pointed etching needle, cutting through the varnish into the surface of the plate; these lines are afterwards corroded with an acid till of a sufficient depth: but before we proceed to the details of the process, we shall describe the various objects which may be wanted, and which are as follows:

Etching-ground This is to be had at all the shops where they sell engraving materials; but for those who wish to make it themselves, the following recipe of Mr Lowry, the celebrated engraver, will be found one of the best. To two ounces of asphaltum add one of Burgundy pitch, and an ounce and a half of white virgin wax. The asphaltum must be finely powdered, and then melted in a glazed earthen vessel over a moderate fire, before the Burgundy pitch is put in; the wax must be added last, when the whole composition must be well stirred, and then poured into warm water, to be further incorporated by means of the hands, and made up into balls. When used, a ball ought to be tied up in a piece of stout silk cloth.

Transparent etching-ground may be made by putting one ounce of common resin and two ounces of virgin wax into a glazed pipkin; set it over a gentle fire until it simmers, and when cool is fit for use, and is laid in the same way as the common etching-ground, except that instead of being smoked it must be warmed with a piece of writing-paper after being dabbed. A very good transparent etching-ground may be made by covering the plate with thin turpentine varnish, in which a small quantity of oxyde of bismuth has been mixed; this should be laid on very evenly with a camel's hair brush, and has the property of showing the original etching in the plate, over which it is laid, much better than the former transparent ground, as it is less dazzling.

A hand-vice, not less than five inches in length, will be wanted to hold the plate while heating it.

Etching needles (Fig 1a) should be three or four different degrees of fineness. To sharpen them well requires some degree of manual dexterity and practice.

The gravers (Fig 1e) should be of different forms, from the extreme lozenge to the square, the lozenge being for fine, and the square for broad lines. To sharpen the belly, or sharp edge of the graver, requires great nicety. Lay one of the flat sides of the graver on the oilstone, keeping the right arm close to the side, and the fore-finger of the left hand pressed upon that side of the graver which is uppermost; next, sharpen the other side the same way. The face or point is sharpened by holding it firm in your hand, with the belly upwards, in a slanting position; then rub it backwards and forwards on the stone, taking care to carry it evenly along, and not to make more than one face on the point; this being done, hold the graver a little more perpendicular to square the point, which will be done in a very short time, as it should not be squared too much.

The scraper (Fig 1b) should be three-sided, and fluted, as they are easier to sharpen: it is used to take off the burr left by the etching needle or dry-point.

The burnisher (Fig 1c) is used to soften lines which have been bit too dark. We recommend the kind used by mezzotint engravers, as being the best form for all kinds of neat and delicate work (Fig 1d).

The oil-rubber should be made of woollen cloth, rolled up as tight as possible, and tied round with string; one, six or seven inches long and two inches or two inches and a half in diameter, is sufficiently large for almost all purposes. Where a small one is wanted, a piece of cloth laid over your fore-finger, may be advantageously used, or a piece of very soft cork will do. The oil-rubber is used with oil alone, or with oil and

Washed flour of Emery which is emery in a state of impalpable powder, and of the greatest use in rubbing down parts that are too dark, as is also

Emery paper, not such as is used by servants to clean iron utensils, but such as is made with washed flour of emery, and like it only to be had, I believe, at some of the great ironmongers, or at some of the coppersmiths.

Charcoal is also used, with either oil or water, in rubbing down dark parts, or taking out blemishes in copper plates: to be procured best at your coppersmith's, who will give you the kind you want.

A camel's hair brush with very long hair will be wanted, to sweep off loose varnish while etching; some small ones for stopping out, and larger ones for laying on transparent ground, and varnishing broad parts of the plate.

The dabber (Fig 1n) to lay the etching ground even, is made by tying up cotton wool very tight in a piece of silk, which should be as even as possible, without any threads larger than the rest. We recommend fine wool instead of cotton wool; and if it is laid very thick on a round piece of card-board, three inches in diameter, and a double silk stretched over it and tied behind, so as to make a soft elastic even cushion, well raised in the middle, it will be found more convenient to handle than the common dabber.

The bridge, or rest, is a thin board planed smooth, with the edges sloped off, and of a length and breadth proportioned to the size of the plate you are working upon. At each end is fastened a piece of wood sufficiently high to raise it above the plate when the wall of wax is on. There should also be another, much lower, to be used in etching, before the wall is made.

The blind, or shade, is made of tissue paper, stretched upon a frame, and placed between your work and the light, to enable you to see better on the surface of the bright copper.

Besides the above-mentioned objects, it is necessary to have a Turkey stone, or hone, a couple of glass bottles with glass stoppers, one of them with a small mouth capable of holding a pound of pure nitrous acid, the other with a wide mouth and capable of containing a pint or more, according to the size of the work which will have to be covered, of diluted nitrous acid. Should architecture form the subject of the plate to be etched, a tee-square, and brass edged parallel

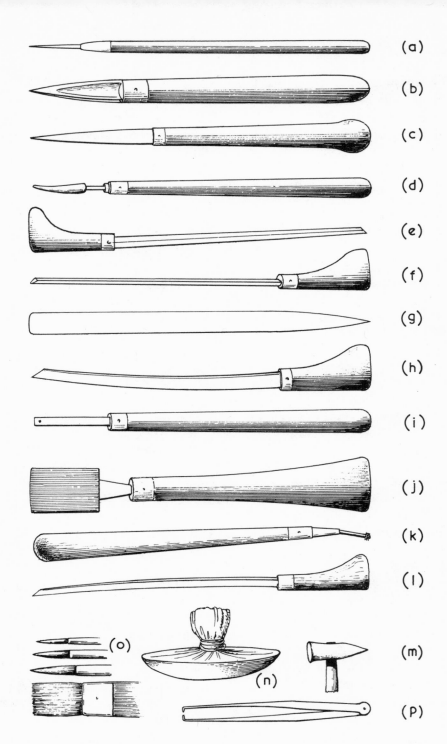

(a)

(b)

(c)

(d)

(e)

(f)

(g)

(h)

(i)

(j)

(k)

(l)

(o)

(n)

(m)

(P)

ruler will be wanted. A pair of steel screw compasses will also be useful for etching arches.

Copper or steel plates are, or ought to be, sufficiently well polished when brought home from the coppersmith's, to admit of having the etching-ground laid upon them without any further preparation; but the former being a softer metal, is extremely liable to get scratched, or the polish destroyed. When this is the case the scratches ought to be burnished, and the burnisher's marks taken out by oil rubbing the plate with washed flour of emery and sweet oil.

Sometimes, however, it happens that the scratch is too deep, or a line or point *bit in* so strongly as not to admit of being effaced either by the burnisher or the scraper. In this case recourse must be had to the process of *knocking up* which we shall briefly describe.

The instruments required are—a polished steel anvil, a hammer (Fig 1m) having a head, with one end flat and the other with a rounded point, and a pair of calliper compasses (Fig 1p). By placing the plate between the legs of the compasses, with one of the points on the spot to be effaced, you can easily mark on the back with the other point the place immediately opposite to it. The plate is then placed with the part to be effaced on the anvil, and struck at the back with the round end of the hammer, till the line or hole is filled up. The jarring of the plate in the hand, and the noise of the hammer, will sufficiently indicate when the part of the surface immediately opposite to where you strike is fairly on the anvil or not. Before, however, you proceed to the actual hammering, the work on the part to be effaced must be carefully taken out with an instrument called a scooper (Fig 1f), so as to leave a clean smooth hollow.

When the part to be effaced is very minute, an iron punch is used, and the plate must then be held on the anvil by an assistant, whilst you hold the punch steadily with the left hand, on the spot marked at the back with the compasses, and strike it gently, but smartly, with the hammer, till the place is filled up.

However neatly the operation of knocking up is performed, the lines of the etching in the immediate vicinity of the part knocked up will be more or less weakened or effaced, and will want re-etching with a transparent ground, or working up to their original strength with the graver. It often happens, also, that the part effaced is raised above the level of the plate, in which case, it must

Fig 1 Etchers' and engravers' tools, after an illustration in T. H. Fielding's *Art of Engraving*: (a) etching needle (b) scraper (c) burnisher (d) burnisher (for mezzotint work) (e) graver (o) burin (f) scooper (g) scraper (for mezzotint work) (h) stipple graver (i) roulette (for mezzotint) (j) shading tool (for mezzotint) (k) roulette (for mezzotint) (l) dry-point or stipple graver (m) hammer (n) dabber (o) brushes (the small ones are red sables, the large, camel hair, for applying broad tints of varnish in aquatint) (p) calliper compasses

be brought down with the scraper, and afterwards finished with the charcoal.

When a new plate has been oil rubbed, the oil is first wiped off with a rag, it is then washed with spirits of turpentine, and after that is wiped off, is cleaned and polished with a dry rag and whiting; it is then ready for an etching-ground, which is laid in the following manner—

Fasten the plate in the hand-vice, and hold it with the surface upwards over a charcoal fire, or heat it with pieces of paper, till so hot that you cannot bear your finger on it; then rub the etching-ground, wrapped up in a piece of silk, backwards and forwards, till the plate is covered as evenly as you can with the ground, which, melting with the heat, oozes through the silk. Next, with the dabber, dab the plate gently all over till it appears of the same colour, as it is darkest on those places where there is most etching-ground, and continue the dabbing till the plate *begins* to cool, and no longer. Then, whilst the ground is yet warm, take a candle, or what is still better, a wax taper twisted together, so that six or more flames unite in one, and cutting the wicks short hold them under the plate turned with the ground downwards, and keep the flame moving backwards and forwards till every part of the ground is of a shining black colour. The greatest care must be taken never to let the flame remain a moment in the same place, as the ground would burn, which is easily seen by its becoming dull and cracked. When cold, the plate is ready for the reception of the design.

As a subject is seldom etched upon a plate at once, without having previously made a picture, or at least an outline on paper, we must now describe the various methods of reducing, tracing, and transferring the tracing on to the plate.

When the picture is larger than the plate on which you intend to copy it, take a pair of compasses and divide the top and bottom into an equal number of parts, marking each part on the edge of the picture with a pencil or chalk; then with the compasses in the same position measure off along the sides of the picture, beginning at the bottom, as many parts as the sides will contain, so that the remainder or fraction of a square, if any, may be at the top. You can now, if an oil painting, draw lines either with a black water colour, which is easily cleaned off afterwards by a spunge, if the picture be light, or white water colour, if dark: or if the subject be a painting in water colours, wrap round it threads from top to bottom, and from side to side; take a piece of smooth writing paper the size of the intended subject (which must always be so much less than the plate, as to leave at least half an inch or more of margin all round) and divide it with a pen and a pale tint of lake or vermilion into exactly the same number of squares as the picture; then with an F, HB, or B pencil, copy whatever is in each square of the picture into the corresponding square on your paper, and to prevent mistakes number the squares both on the painting and the paper. This being done, damp the paper well, fix it with the face downwards on the etching-ground with wax at one side, and let the printer pass it through a moderately tight rolling-press, by which means the pencil marks will be transferred to the ground, so that the subject will appear *reversed*, in fine silvery lines.

When the subject you mean to copy is to be the same size on the plate, take a piece of thick transparent tracing paper, and fastening it firmly to the painting by turning a part of it over the top and pasting it behind, trace the outline with a blacklead pencil, and then transfer it to the ground as directed above.

When no rolling-press is to be had, another method must be pursued to transfer the outline to the etching-ground. Having made the tracing or reduction on *thin* transparent paper, take a piece of the thinnest and smoothest foreign letter paper, or a piece of glazed tissue paper, and rub it evenly over with vermilion, chrome yellow, white lead, or any other light colour in impalpable powder till well covered. Then having turned down the tracing on to the plate, and fastened it with wax at the top edge, place the vermilion paper between it and the ground with the colour side downwards, and with a blunt pointed etching needle, called a tracing point, go over the outline using a moderate pressure, by which means it will be transferred in colour to the etching-ground. A still quicker method is often used, but which requires the greatest delicacy as well as firmness of touch, and a tracing point perfectly rounded so as not to cut the paper and so injure the ground, is to rub the front of the tracing itself with vermilion, and lay it on the plate so as to do away with the necessity of an intermediate coloured paper.

The bridge being placed over it, the plate is now ready for the commencement of the etching. The etching needles with the most tapering points should be used for the skies and distance, pressing more heavily, and changing them for others as we approach the foreground, sharpened, with a thicker point made by holding it more perpendicularly on the stone, so as to give a broader and deeper line. Wherever the ruler is used for buildings, ship-masts, &c., it is to be remembered that the lines made with it will be much darker than those made by the hand, so that a much less pressure is required. Wherever any error has been made the part must be covered evenly, and not too thickly, with a camel's hair pencil dipped in Brunswick black, and when dry the lines re-etched *through* it. We must here remark that the etching must always penetrate so well *through* the etching-ground as to scratch the metal; and when the plate is steel, it is better, as much as possible, to avoid breathing upon it, as the slightest humidity will often rust it.

Though the shade sides of white objects may generally be etched and bit in with aquafortis, it is better to do them with the dry point, which is peculiarly well adapted for the fur and hair of white animals, the light of white drapery, light clouds and sky, and extreme distances.

The etching being finished, the plate must be carefully examined, and all accidental scratches stopped out with Brunswick black. When this is dry, a wall or border is put round the plate, which is done by softening the bordering wax in warm water till perfectly ductile; it is then pulled out into straps about six inches long, one inch broad, and a quarter of an inch thick, and the edge pressed down immediately before it cools on the margin, and the thumb of the left hand passed along the inner edge with a strong pressure so as to squeeze the wax close down to the plate: another piece is to be immediately joined to the first, and so on till the plate is surrounded, leaving a spout at one corner to pour off the acid.

It is difficult to give exact rules for *biting in*, but the following will be found sufficient. Procure some strong nitrous acid, and such is sold by Mr Sellers the Chemist, in Broad Street, St Giles's, at a shilling the pound, and then mix, in a wide-mouthed bottle, one part of the acid with five parts of water, adding to it a small portion of sal ammoniac, in the proportion of the size of a hazel nut, to one pint of acid, when mixed for *biting*. Pour the mixture, *when cool* (nitrous acid becoming warm when mixed with water), on to the plate, and leave it to bite in the delicate parts about a quarter of an hour, sweeping off the bubbles as they form on the plate with an old camel's hair brush or feather; take off the acid, wash the plate with water, and dry it either by blowing with bellows, or pressing on it gently with a piece of blotting paper; stop out with Brunswick black those parts which are sufficiently bit in; again put on the acid, let it remain twenty minutes or half an hour, to give the next degree of depth; wash and stop out as before, and leave the acid on for half or three quarters of an hour for the last biting, as three bites are generally sufficient for most painters' etching.

The wall is now to be taken off by warming the margin of the plate at the back with a piece of lighted paper; it is then to be washed clean with spirits of turpentine, then oil rubbed, then again washed with spirits, and after being wiped dry may be taken to the printer's for a proof.

The process of biting in, described above, is only applicable to copper plates: for steel plates another method is pursued, which is as follows:—

Mix together

Pyroligneous acid   ..   ..   1 part

| Nitric acid | .. | .. | .. | .. | .. | 1 part |
| Water | .. | .. | .. | .. | .. | 6 parts |

In *biting in* with this composition the first tint will be only on and off, washing the plate immediately with water, and never using the same water twice; when washed, the plate must be set on one edge, and blown dry with bellows as soon as possible to prevent rusting.

In biting in steel, one minute will be generally found long enough for the darkest tint.

If, on examining the proof, all or part of the etching is found too weak, it may be made stronger either by etching over it with a transparent ground, or, when the tint is not too delicate, by rebiting, in which case a rebiting ground must be laid, and which is performed in the following manner.

Clean the plate well with spirits of turpentine, then wash it with pure water of potass, next rinse the plate with perfectly clean water several times, till entirely free from the potass, and wipe it quite dry with a clean rag. This being done, heat a spare piece of copper or steel plate, on which melt some etching-ground, then with a silk dabber (a new one is best) take up a small quantity, and having previously heated the plate which is to be rebit, dab it very lightly all over, and continue till every part of the surface is well covered with the ground, leaving the lines perfectly clear. This is an operation which requires great patience and the utmost delicacy of touch, and as it takes considerable time, the plate must be heated very often to keep up the same degree of warmth, which is extremely difficult. For this reason it is better to employ the following method, which is now generally used by most engravers not only for rebiting, but also for common etching-grounds. Procure a tin box twelve inches long, nine broad, and three deep, without any opening except a hole at one corner, by which it is to be filled with hot water. This is placed on a stand so as to admit of a small charcoal stove underneath, by which the water must always be kept at a boiling heat. The plate is laid on this box, and by this means kept at an uniform temperature, so that there is no danger of burning the ground, which so often happens when the plate is heated in the common way. When the ground is cold, a wall may be put round it, and the subject bit in as before.

A well-practised etcher, after each biting in, takes off a very small portion of the ground, and can then judge in what manner it will print. He then stops out, or passes over all the lines which may be sufficiently deep, with Brunswick black, and proceeds with the rest as we have already mentioned.

When any line or small part is too dark, it may be made lighter with the burnisher; but when any broad tint or the whole of the plate is too dark, the quickest way is to rub it down with the emery paper before mentioned. This, however, should be well rubbed on a piece of copper or steel, to take off the sharpness which might otherwise scratch, and even then it will leave a mark, which would show strongly in the proof if not first taken out with soft charcoal and oil, and then polished with the oil rubber.

A pleasing way of giving more effect to an etching, when finished, is to take off the polish of the plate with the emery paper, by which means a delicate tint is laid all over it, and on which the lights on clouds, white figures, water, &c., may be burnished. Pumice stone finely powdered and sifted through muslin, and rubbed on with a rag will do the same; and Rembrandt often, by leaving the surface of the plate only partially cleaned from the printing ink, when proving, produced a singular effect on some of his etchings.

When etching or engraving by lamp light, we recommend the use of a globe of water, placed between the lamp and the plate, as described under the head of Wood Engraving.

SOFT-GROUND ETCHING

Etching on soft ground is a style of engraving formerly much employed to imitate chalk or pencil drawings. Since the invention of lithography, however, it has been almost entirely abandoned, though for those who live too far from any town, where a lithographic press is established, it will be found a great source of amusement.

Soft ground for winter use is made by adding one part of hog's lard, to three parts of common etching-ground; but for warm weather, less hog's lard is required. The ground is laid and smoked in the same way as the hard etching-ground, taking care that nothing touches it after it is done, till the paper is laid on.

The process is as follows. Draw the outline of your subject faintly on a piece of smooth thin writing paper, which must be at least an inch larger every way than the plate; then damp it, and spread it cautiously on the ground, and turning the edges over, paste them down to the back of the plate: in a few hours the paper will be dry, and stretched quite smooth. Resting your hand on the bridge take an H or HB pencil, and draw your subject on the paper exactly as you wish it to be, pressing strongly for the darker touches, and more lightly for the more delicate parts, and according as you find the ground more or less soft, which depends on the heat of the weather, or the room you work in, use a softer or harder pencil, remembering always that the softer the ground the softer the pencil. When the drawing is finished lift up the paper carefully from the plate, and wherever you have touched with the pencil the ground will stick to the paper, leaving the copper more or less exposed. A wall is then put round the margin, the plate bit in, and if too feeble, rebit in the same way as a common etching, using *hard etching-ground* for the rebite. If the acid has been successfully applied to the plate the proof will be exactly the same as the drawing made by the soft etching-ground sticking to the underside of the paper, which is indeed itself a proof how far you have succeeded.

LINE ENGRAVING

Of all the various kinds of engraving, the art we are about to describe stands pre-eminently the first. However it may be surpassed by other branches of the profession in the representation of certain objects, yet as a whole it is decidedly superior to the rest. It cannot produce the velvety softness, intense depth, and harmonious mingling of light and shade, which is given by mezzotint. Neither can it, even when aided by the ruling machine, produce that silvery clearness, or deep transparent tone perceived in aquatint; nor like it, reproduce the *dragging, scumbling*, and accidental touches of the artist's brush. In crispness and brilliancy it is far exceeded by wood engraving. Still it stands before all others, and we cannot but see with regret, though not surprise, its present declining state.

The process of line engraving consists at present, in first etching the plate, and then after it is bitten in, finishing it with the graver and dry point. Formerly, however, it was the custom to begin and finish a plate with the graver only; but this method has long been laid aside, as the use of the etching needle gives so much greater freedom in the representation of almost every object.

Of the method of laying the ground, transferring the subject to the plate by means of tracing, and of sharpening the graver, needle, &c, we have already spoken under the head of etching. The manner of handling the needle is, however, very different, as in all the flat tints a ruler is made use of. Clear blue skies are done by means of the ruling machine, of which the following is a description. On a straight bar of steel is placed a socket, which slides backwards and forwards with a steady, but even motion. To the side of the socket is fitted a perpendicular tube, which receives a steel wire or any other hard substance, called a pen. This pen has a point like an etching needle, and is pressed down by the action of a spring. If, then, a copper plate covered with the etching-ground is placed under the ruler, which should be supported at each end, and raised about an inch above it, the point of the pen may be caused to reach it; and if the socket to which the pen is attached be drawn along the bar, it will form a straight line upon the plate, more even, but in other respects the same as if that line had been drawn by hand with a ruler. Now, if the plate or the ruler be moved, backwards or forwards, in a direction parallel to this first line, any number of lines may be drawn in the same manner.

In the machine, therefore, a very exact screw, acting upon a box confined by a slide and connected with the bar or board upon which the plate rests, produces the requisite motion; and a contrivance or index is used to measure the exact portion of a turn required before any stroke is drawn. Such is the principle of the machine most generally used; but the point or pen employed should not be made of steel, which however well tempered will require frequent sharpening, and must therefore inevitably draw strokes deficient in perfect uniformity. The pen should have a diamond point, which when once properly figured remains constantly the same, and imparts an admirable degree of regularity and sweetness to the work.

Though the ruler is used in laying flat tints, it does not follow that the lines made with it are to be straight; on the contrary, they are made to take the form most suited to the object by slightly moving the hand, taking care to make them parallel. But the greatest difficulty, and what requires the longest practice to attain, is to give that equal pressure to the needle, so that every line may be the same depth, width, and distance from each other, without which it is entirely hopeless to obtain an even tint. This capability of laying flat tints, and of ruling parallel lines excessively close without running into each other, is so essential, that no one can expect to make a decent plate till he has fully accomplished it; and the first business of the learner should be by continual practice to obtain a readiness and certainty in the management of the ruler and needle. He must also be equally capable of laying parallel lines of the same strength without the aid of the ruler, and must seek to acquire a freedom of handling in etching grass and the foliage of trees in landscape, and the flowing lines required in drapery and the waves of the sea.

The following extracts from a celebrated work on Engraving, aided by the examination of the prints of the best professors of the art, will be found worthy of attention. The strokes of the graver should never be crossed too much in the lozenge manner, particularly in the representation of flesh, because sharp angles produce the unpleasing effect of lattice work, and take from the eye the repose which is agreeable to it in all kinds of picturesque designs; we should except the case of clouds, tempests, waves of the sea, the skins of hairy animals, or the leaves of trees, where this method of crossing may be admitted. But in avoiding the lozenge it is not proper to get entirely into the square, which would give too much of the hardness of stone. In conducting the strokes, the action of the figures and of all their parts should be considered, and it should be observed how they advance towards, or recede from the eye, and the graver should be guided according to the risings or cavities of the muscles or folds, making the strokes wider and fainter in the lights, and closer and firmer in the shades. Thus the figures will not appear jagged, and the hand should be lightened in such a manner, that the outlines may be formed and terminated without being cut too hard; however, though the strokes break off where the muscle begins, yet they ought always to have a certain connection with each other, so that the first stroke may often serve by its return to make the second, which will show the freedom of the engraver.

When architecture is to be represented, except it be old and ruinous buildings, the work ought not to be made very black, because as edifices are commonly constructed either of stone or white marble, the colour being reflected on all sides does not produce dark shades as in other substances.

In engraving architecture, the strokes which form the rounding of objects should tend to the point of sight, and when whole columns occur, it is proper to produce the effect as much as possible by perpendicular strokes. If a cross stroke is put, it should be at right angles, and wider and thinner than the first stroke. The strokes ought to be frequently discontinued and broken for sharp and craggy objects. Objects that are distant, towards the horizon should be kept very tender. Waters that are calm and still, are best represented by strokes that are straight and parallel to the horizon, interlined with those that are finer, omitting such places as in consequence of gleams of light exhibit the shining appearance of water; and the forms of objects reflected upon the water at a small distance from it, or on the banks of the water, are expressed by the same strokes retouched more strongly or faintly as occasion may require, and even by some that are perpendicular. For agitated waters, as the waves of the sea, the first strokes should follow the figure of the waves, and may be interlined, and the cross strokes ought to be very lozenge. In cascades, the strokes should follow the fall and be interlined. In engraving clouds, the graver or needle should sport where they appear thick and agitated, in turning every way according to their form and their agitation. If the clouds are dark so that two strokes are necessary, they should be crossed more lozenge than the figures, and the second strokes should be rather wider than the first. The flat clouds that are lost insensibly in the clear sky should be made by strokes parallel to the horizon, and a little waving; if second strokes are required ,they should be more or less lozenge, and when they are brought to the extremity the hand should be so lightened that they may form no outline. The flat and clear sky is represented by parallel and straight strokes, without the least turning. In landscapes, the trees, rocks, earth, herbage, and indeed every part except white objects, should be etched as much as possible; nothing should be left for the graver, but perfecting, softening, and strengthening.

The above observations will be found very useful to refer to, though perhaps after all, the examination of the prints of the best engravers will be found the best instruction that the beginner can have; but then that examination ought to be, not merely to see how certain work is performed, but the manner of executing the representation of the same object by different engravers should be carefully observed, and that which is best selected as a model, remarking at the same time wherein consists its excellence, and in what manner it differs from the rest.

WOOD ENGRAVING

The process of wood engraving is exactly the reverse of engraving on steel or copper, in which the portions of the print required to be left white remain untouched, while the black and tinted parts are produced by a series of lines cut out of the metal with the graver; whereas in wood the black and tinted portions are left even with the surface, and the white parts are cut out. Whilst the engraver on steel produces his effect by a series of incised lines, the wood engraver cuts away only that part not intended to print.

In printing wood blocks it is necessary that the ink used should be of a composition much thicker than that employed in the production of prints from engravings on copper or steel, in order that it may lie *upon* the surface of the block without filling up the hollows. The manner in which type is printed is so well known, that it is only necessary to say that the printing of wood blocks is exactly similar, and generally done at the same time, as they are chiefly used in the illustration of books.

There are three kinds of wood used in this style of engraving; Sycamore, Pear, and Box, the two former being only used for large coarse cuts, such as are often seen at the head of play bills, as they are too soft to admit of fine lines being engraved upon them.

Box wood is grown in England, and though not so large as that imported from America or the Levant, is equally good or perhaps better, rarely of a red colour, which is a certain sign of softness and of course unfitness for fine work, for which the smallest logs should always be chosen, those blocks which are of a clear yellow colour *all over* being the best. This however is very difficult to obtain, as almost always the centre of the tree is of a deeper yellow than the outside, which is in general whitish and much softer.

Box is purchased in small trunks varying from four to twelve or fourteen inches in diameter, and from two to five feet in length; they are cut into slices of about seven-eighths of an inch in thickness, the same as that of type in order that the engraving may be printed simultaneously with the letter-press. These slices after being cut from the trunk are laid by for a period varying according to circumstances, from twelve months to two years, to ensure their being properly seasoned.

To prepare a block for drawing, nothing more is requisite than to cover the smooth surface with a thin coating of Bath brick finely powdered, and mixed with a little water, which when dry is to be removed by rubbing it off with the palm of the hand. This gives a certain degree of roughness which makes the blacklead pencil mark more freely on the block. Drawings on wood are executed in two different styles. One in which the principal flat tints are *laid in* in Indian ink, and then touched up with a blacklead pencil; the other in which every line is drawn exactly as it is intended to be produced in the engraving, the facsimile style as it is called, and which is much easier, and requires less skill in the engraver to execute than the former.

The tools used by wood engravers, are gravers, tint tools, scoopers or gouges, chisels or flat tools, and a mezzotint scraper (Fig 1g) for scraping away the wood in the process of lowering. The gravers are the same as those used in line engraving, and vary in form from the square lozenge (Fig 2a) to the extreme lozenge (Fig 2b). Six or eight will generally be found sufficient.

Tint tools (Fig 2c) are deeper in the sides than gravers, and are used where a succession of fine parallel lines are wanted. Six will be found sufficient, those for the broadest lines being about as fine as the most lozenge graver, the five others growing gradually finer.

Scoopers (Fig 1f) are chiefly used for scooping out the wood from the middle parts of the block, and ought to be of six different sizes.

Flat tools, chisels, or as they are sometimes called blocking out tools (Fig 2d), are used for cutting away those parts of the block which are towards the sides after the engraving is finished.

When the drawing is finished, the block is placed on a sand bag, which being higher in the centre, allows it to be turned with more facility, and thereby gives greater freedom of execution.

In all those parts of the drawing which are meant to be extremely soft and light, the surface of the block should be lowered before the engraver begins to work upon it. As of course this operation, which is done with a mezzotint scraper, entirely effaces those parts of the design on which it is performed, and which the engraver must either draw in again himself or take it back to the artist, it is much better that only an outline be made at first, and the parts to be lowered indicated with tints of white colour. The wood engraver proceeds to

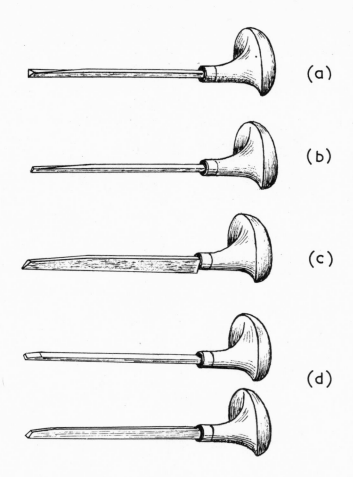

Fig 2 Wood engravers' tools, after an illustration in T. H. Fielding's *Art of Engraving*: (a) square lozenge (b) extreme lozenge (c) tint tool (d) flat or blocking out tools, or chisels

lower the block in the necessary places, and then gives it back to the draughts-man who finishes his drawing. By these means there is less danger of the drawing being injured during the process, but at the same time it requires that the artist should perfectly understand the principle of lowering.

It is in those designs which are made on the block with Indian ink, that the mechanical skill and artistical powers of the engraver are fully shown. Left almost entirely to himself, the choice of the kind of work with which he proposes to make out the different parts of the drawing, depends more on his knowledge as a draughtsman than his skill in handling the graver: for instance, let an Indian ink drawing of a fox be given to two engravers, one of whom shall be eminent for the cleverness with which he can manage his tools, and the other very deficient in this respect, but at the same time more used to the drawing of animals, the latter shall produce an engraving, which however roughly executed will have that resemblance to nature, for the want of which no skill or beauty of execution on the part of the former can compensate.

When the engraving is finished, a proof is obtained in the following manner. With a small silk dabber dipt in printing ink, the whole surface of the block is evenly covered by dabbing it with a light steady hand, and not too much ink, so as not to force it *between* the lines. A piece of India paper is next laid on the block with a card over it to prevent the fine lines from being injured by the pressure. A burnisher is then rubbed firmly all over, by which an impression of the work is taken off on to the India paper.

When an injury has happened to any part of the work, the only remedy is to introduce a fresh piece of wood: for this purpose a circular hole is drilled nearly through the block, sufficiently large to cut out the part to be obliterated; a plug of box is then driven in, and the part re-engraved.

One of the greatest advantages which wood engraving possesses over all other kinds, is the facility with which the same block may be multiplied by means of stereotyping. This is done in two ways. The first is by taking a mould of the block in plaster of Paris, from which a cast is made in type metal, and this, if the operation has been carefully performed, will be very little inferior to the block itself. The second method is by impressing the surface of the block in melted metal, sufficiently liquid to receive the impression: from this mould a cast is taken, but this method, notwithstanding the metal cools immediately the block is placed upon it, is very dangerous, as the finer lines of the wood engraving are extremely liable to become charred, though the whole surface of the wood be previously rubbed with soap.

In engraving on wood by lamplight, a most excellent method is to place between the work and the lamp a glass globe filled with clear water, in such a manner that the concentrated rays of light may fall upon the block. This has the advantage of giving a much more brilliant light than the lamp itself, and at the same time much cooler, as the lamp is at a greater distance. It is also much more economical, as a single lamp will serve several persons each having a globe.

Chiaoscuro drawings are easily imitated on wood by printing over the impression of the finished engraving a second block with the high lights cut out: this, if printed in grey ink, will give the appearance of a pen and ink drawing done on grey paper, with the high light touched in with white colour; and by using several blocks with different colours Mr Baxter has been enabled to produce beautifully finished impressions in oil colours, as may be seen in the Pictorial Album of 1837.

AQUATINT

Aquatint is a complicated process and Fielding's description is both lengthy and detailed. The method which he followed himself, and which had been practised by Burdett and Sandby, involved dissolving resin in spirits of wine and pouring the liquid over a highly polished copper plate. The plate is warmed and the spirit evaporates, leaving a granulated surface on the plate, known as the ground. Usually the outline of the subject is etched onto the plate before the ground is applied and the etched lines filled with ink. Sometimes the subject was traced or drawn onto the plate.

When all is ready, the plate is exposed to acid which bites around the resin granules. As each required tone is reached, the plate is withdrawn and the area of tone covered with a stopping-out varnish. This continues until the darkest tones are obtained, possibly eight or twelve 'bites' being required. As Fielding says, 'engraving in aquatint is like making an Indian ink drawing: each time the aquafortis is put on the plate a fresh tint is produced, and as each part successively becomes dark enough, it is stopped out'.

Another method of laying the ground was that patented by Jean Baptiste Le Prince in 1768, in which the warmed plate was coated with powdered resin. The powder might be applied by being shaken on from a muslin bag, or the plate itself might be inserted in a dust-box in which the powder is circulated by means of a fan or bellows. Fielding says that by his time this method was no longer employed in England, but it has come back into use in recent years.

The 'sugar-lift' method was also used. In this, the whole plate is varnished after the subject has been brushed on with a mixture of sugar and Indian ink. When the plate is washed in warm water the mixture dissolves, leaving the design exposed on the plate. Gainsborough was one of the first English artists to experiment with the 'sugar-lift' method.

Aquatint plates could be printed uncoloured or in one or two coloured inks. Coloured aquatints were finished by hand, and the best examples are difficult to distinguish from water-colour paintings. A wide range of effects could be obtained, from Samuel Alken's softly tinted plates after Gilpin to the brilliance of Reeve's fully coloured interpretations of the drawings of William Westall and Samuel Owen. But as we have seen, the major disadvantage of the coloured aquatint was the cost of production; long print-runs were impractical and it had almost ceased to be used in England by the mid-nineteenth century.

LITHOGRAPHY

Lithography—the art of writing and drawing on stone—depends on the natural antipathy which grease and water have for each other. Basically the process is simple, although it is capable of a large number of developments and refinements. The stone used in the earlier years, by Senefelder and Hullmandel, was limestone from Bavaria but other sources were found in the nineteenth century, including quarries near Bath.

After the surface of the stone has been smoothed, washed and dried, a drawing in lithographic chalk or ink is made directly onto it. Both the chalk and ink are greasy. The stone is then washed over and printing ink applied with a roller. This ink affixes to the greased image but is repelled by the remainder of the wet stone. The image can then be taken off on a sheet of damp paper. The image can also be transferred to the prepared stone by means of transfer paper.

In 1840 the lithotint process was patented; in this a second stone, known as a tint-stone, was used so that the effect of a wash drawing could be obtained. The tint was usually buff or grey. Intermediate tints could be obtained by scraping away. By using several stones, fully coloured impressions were obtainable. And as with aquatints, lithographs could also have colour added by hand.

When Fielding wrote his treatise, zinc plates were coming into use. They enable the most beautiful work, quite equal to lithography, to be produced, he wrote, adding that 'the portability of zinc plates, when compared with the ponderous stones required for large drawings in lithography would always cause them to be preferred, were it not for the circumstance that nothing that is once done can be effaced and again retouched'. He recommended that zincography should only be practised by a skilled and confident artist.

BOOKS
ILLUSTRATED WITH
PRINTS

Unless it is rigidly confined to studies of a particular and limited area, any list of books illustrated with prints is bound to be arbitrary—the larger the area the more arbitrary the list. Some idea of the problem can be gained from J. V. Somers Cocks' *Devonshire Topographical Prints*, which lists 3,502 items, from 229 sources, with over three hundred engravers, etchers and lithographers and about the same number of artists. And this is for only one English county. In front of me is a good antiquarian bookseller's catalogue of British topography and local history; it includes 2,751 publications, at least half of which are illustrated and, of course, it represents only those titles which the bookseller had in stock at one particular moment. Few printsellers issue catalogues—for one thing, only the larger firms would have the staff available to compile them —but one that I have by me contains 1,495 items comprising single prints, sets, books and maps. Moreover, these are prints of quality and comparative rarity, not recently hand-coloured steel engravings after Allom, Bartlett or Westall.

The following book-lists, then, are admittedly arbitrary. They make no claim to include all the volumes illustrated by copper and steel engravings, aquatints, etchings and lithographs that were published in the period we are surveying. Those listed are not necessarily the best examples—who is to say which are the best? But they are, within reason, representative, and that is the only claim that is made. For further research into aquatint, lithography and colour-plate books generally the bibliographies of Abbey and Tooley are most helpful, though neither is comprehensive; so far there is no equivalent for line-engraved work.

Some of the collections are referred to in the text or in the lists of artists and engravers, but I have not thought it necessary to repeat in the reference section all the items mentioned in the preceding chapters. For further details of prints issued singly or in smaller sets you should consult the specialist department of a major library, the appropriate County Record Office, the print room of a museum or gallery or a knowledgeable dealer; if Devon is your county, then Mr Somers Cocks' book is invaluable, and it is to be hoped that others will follow the way he has shown. An enormous amount of work remains to be done on this whole subject.

The great county histories, like Hutchins' *Dorset*, Chauncy's *Hertfordshire*, Polwhele's *Devonshire* and Ormerod's *Chester* have not been included in this list although they are all illustrated with engravings. These volumes should be the subject of a separate survey and I think it inappropriate to consider them merely for their plates alone.

ENGLAND

Ackermann, J. *Microcosm of London*, London 1810. 154 coloured aquatints after A. Pugin and Rowlandson, mostly by Bluck and Stadler

— — *University of Oxford*, London 1814. 64 coloured aquatints after Pugin, Mackenzie, Nash and Westall, by Bluck, Stadler, Sutherland and others

— — *University of Cambridge*, London 1815. 64 coloured aquatints after Pugin, Mackenzie and Westall by the same team of engravers. See text for further details

Amsinck, P. *Tunbridge Wells and its Neighbourhood*, 1810. With 43 etched plates by Letitia Byrne

Angus, W. *The Seats of the Nobility and Gentry*, W. Angus, Islington 1787-1810. 60 copper engraved plates by Angus after Dayes, Malton, Paul and Thomas Sandby, Repton and others

Arnout, J. *Grande Bretagne, Angleterre, Ecosse, Irlande*, Gambart & Co, London (c 1855). 40 fine tinted lithographs

Barber, T. *Picturesque Illustrations of the Isle of Wight*, London 1835. 41 steel engraved plates, mostly after Bartlett but a few after Barber, engraved by Barber, Fisher and H. Winkles

Boydell, J. *A Collection of Views in England and Wales*, London 1790. Drawn and engraved by Boydell

Brannon, G. Several volumes on the Isle of Wight, drawn, engraved and published by the Brannon family. See text

Brewer, J. N. *The Picture of England*, London 1821. In two volumes with over two hundred and fifty copper engravings

Britton, J. *The Architectural Antiquities of Great Britain*, London 1807-26. Five volumes with engravings after Sandby, Repton, Prout, Nash and others

— — *Picturesque Views of the English Cities*, London 1828. Engraved after drawings by G. F. Robson

— — *Picturesque Antiquities of the English Cities*, London 1830. With 60 copper engraved plates

Britton, J., Brayley, E. W., Brewer, J. *The Beauties of England and Wales*, London 1801–8. Twenty-six volumes, with 684 engraved plates by and after a wide variety of artists. See text

Buck, S. and N. *Views of Ruins of Castles and Abbeys in England and Wales*, London 1726–42. Two volumes first published by the Bucks and republished by Sayer as *Buck's Antiquities*, 1774. 420 plates

Byrne, W. *Britannia Depicta*, London 1806–18. Copper engravings by Byrne of the most interesting and picturesque objects in Great Britain, first published in 6 parts

— — *Antiquities of Great Britain*, London 1807. Two volumes of views of monasteries, castles and churches engraved by Byrne after the drawings of Thomas Hearne, with descriptions in English and French

Calvert, F. *Picturesque Views, and Descriptions of Cities, Towns, Castles, Mansions . . . in Staffordshire and Shropshire*, Birmingham 1830. 37 engravings by Radclyffe after Calvert, with text by William West

Calvert, F. and Roberts, P. *The Isle of Wight Illustrated*, 1846. With 20 coloured aquatints drawn by Calvert and engraved by Roberts

Clarke, E. D. *A Tour through the South of England, Wales and Part of Ireland*, London 1793. With 11 uncoloured aquatints

Cooke, G. *Views in London and its Vicinity*, London 1834. 48 copper engravings by George Cooke from drawings by Callcott, Stanfield, Prout, Roberts, Stark, Harding, Cotman, Havell and others, after original sketches made on the spot by Edward W. Cooke

Cooke, W. *A New Picture of the Isle of Wight, Illustrated . . .*, Southampton 1812. 26 plates drawn and engraved by William Cooke

Cooke, W. B. and G. *Thames Scenery*, London 1818. Two volumes with 75 etched and engraved plates by the Cookes

Cosmo *Travels of Cosmo the Third, Grand Duke of Tuscany, through England . . .* (1669), London 1821. Text translated from the Italian of L. Magalotti. 39 sepia aquatints by T. H. Shepherd, after drawings made by an Italian artist during the tour

Cuitt, G. *Wanderings and Pencillings amongst Ruins of the Olden Time*, 1855. 73 etchings by George Cuitt, who published collections of etchings in 1823, 1834 and 1838

Daniell, W. and Ayton, R. *A Voyage round Great Britain*, London 1814-25.

Eight volumes in four, with 308 coloured aquatints and one uncoloured. See text for further details of this, possibly the finest of the coloured aquatint collections

Davey, H. *A Series of Etchings Illustrative of the Architectural Antiquities of Suffolk*, Southwold 1827

Excursions through Norfolk, London 1818-19. Two volumes containing 96 small engravings after J. S. Cotman by a large variety of engravers. A similar set was published on Suffolk

Farington, J. *Views of Cities and Towns in England and Wales*, London 1790. Issued in three parts

— — *Views and Scenery on the River Thames*, London 1794-6. With 76 coloured aquatints by Stadler after Farington, and text by William Combe

— — *The Lakes of Lancashire, Westmorland and Cumberland*, London 1816. 43 engravings by Byrne, Medland, Pouncy and others after Farington's drawings. Text by T. H. Horne

Fielding, T. H. *Cumberland, Westmorland and Lancashire Illustrated*, London 1822. 44 coloured aquatints after Fielding

— — *British Castles*, London 1822-4. 25 coloured aquatints

Fielding, T. H. and Walton, J. *A Picturesque Tour of the English Lakes*, London 1821. With 48 coloured aquatints by T. H. Fielding after drawings by himself and by J. Walton. This is one of the finest of the Lake District books

Finden, E. and W. *Views of Ports, Harbours, Watering Places. . . .* First published in 1838 by Charles Tilt with 49 steel-engraved plates by the Findens after Creswick, Balmer, Harding, E. W. Cooke, Duncan, Howse, Boys, H. Warren and Nash. Extended edition published by Virtue, 1842, in two volumes with extra plates after W. H. Bartlett engraved by Armytage, Mossman, Varrall, Brandard, Bradshaw, Higham, Wallis, Bentley and a few others; total 124 plates. Further extended in 1874 with some Irish views to make a total of 142. The Findens' *Ports and Harbours* is one of the most popular steel-engraved publications and has been reproduced in the 1970s

Fisher, T. *Collections Historical, Genealogical and Topographical for Bedfordshire*, London 1812-36. 114 copper engravings by or under the direction of Thomas Fisher

Gainsborough, T. *A Collection of Prints, Illustrative of English Scenery*, London 1819. A set of soft-ground etchings by W. F. Wells and J. Laporte (some in colour in some issues) after drawings and sketches by Gainsborough

Gilpin, Revd W. *Observations . . . in the Mountains and Lakes of Cumberland and Westmorland*, London 1786. Two volumes with tinted aquatints after Gilpin

Grose, F. *Antiquities of England, Wales, Scotland and Ireland*, London 1785-97.

Twelve volumes with over one thousand engravings. Francis Grose and Thomas Astle also compiled *The Antiquarian Repertory*. An enlarged edition illustrated with 238 engravings was published London 1807–9, several years after Grose's death.

Harding, J. D. *Harding's Portfolio*, London c1830. 24 hand-coloured lithographs printed by Hullmandel after Harding. For Harding's other publications see text and 'Painters' section

Harral, T. and Ireland, S. *Picturesque Views of the Severn*, London 1824. Two volumes, with 52 lithographs by Calvert after Ireland

Hassell, J. For a list of his books see under 'Painters'

Havell, R. *A Series of Picturesque Views of Noblemen's and Gentlemen's Seats*, London 1823. With 20 coloured aquatints by Robert Havell and Son after W. Havell, C. F. Fielding and others

Havell, W. *A Series of Picturesque Views on the River Thames*, London 1812. 12 coloured aquatints by his brothers Robert and Daniel after William Havell's drawings

Howlett, B. *A Selection of Views in the County of Lincoln*, London 1813. 50 engravings by Howlett after drawings by Girtin, Nattes, Nash, Bourne and others

Ingram, J. *Memorials of Oxford*, Oxford and London 1837. 101 engravings by John Le Keux after drawings by F. Mackenzie

Ireland, S. *Picturesque Views on the River Thames*, London 1792. Two volumes, with 52 sepia aquatints by C. Apostool after Ireland. The plates are coloured in some issues

— — *Picturesque Views on the River Medway*, London 1793. 28 plates as above

— — *Picturesque Views, on the Upper or Warwickshire Avon*, London 1795. 29 plates as above

Jones' *Views of the Seats, Mansions, Castles etc . . . in England, Wales, Scotland and Ireland*, London 1829–30. Contains 196 views

Lysons, D. and S. *Magna Britannia*, London 1806–22. Six volumes published (Bedfordshire to Devonshire) with a total of 263 etched plates

Martineau, H. *The English Lakes*, London 1858. With woodcuts by W. J. Linton, 8 steel engravings by Apsland and Pettit, and 2 chromolithographs by Leighton

Middiman, S. *Select Views in Great Britain*, London 1814. The first edition has 53 engravings by Middiman after Ibbetson, Callandar, Ireland, Wheatley and others

Neale, J. P. *Views of the Seats of Noblemen and Gentlemen in England, Wales, Scotland and Ireland*, London 1818–23. Six volumes, followed by a second series of five more volumes 1824–9

Pennant, T. *The Journey from Chester to London*, London 1782. With 22 engravings. This is only one of Pennant's many *Journeys* and *Tours*

Phillips, J. *The Rivers, Mountains and Sea-Coast of Yorkshire*, London 1853. With 35 lithograph plates

Preston, J. *The Picture of Yarmouth*, 1819. With 19 coloured aquatints after Preston by C. Sloman, I. Clark and others

Pyne, J. B. *Lake Scenery of England*, London 1859. 24 lithographs, and engravings in the text

Pyne, W. H. *The History of the Royal Residences*, London 1819. With 100 coloured aquatints after Wild, Cattermole and others by Sutherland, Reeve and other engravers

Radclyffe, C. *Picturesque Antiquities of the County of Hereford*, Hereford c1845. With 32 tinted lithographs

Radclyffe, W. and T. *Graphic Illustrations of Warwickshire*, Birmingham 1829. With 64 plates and 12 vignettes after Westall, Radclyffe, Harding, de Wint and others

Raye, Charles *A Picturesque Tour through the Isle of Wight*, London 1825. 24 coloured plates (23 aquatint, 1 etched), 2 signed as engraver by C. Rosenberg. Very attractive

Russell, P. and Price, O. *England Displayed*, London 1769. Two volumes, with 81 copper engraved plates in picture frame borders; also 54 maps

Sandby, Paul *A Collection of 150 Select Views in England, Wales, Scotland and Ireland*, London 1782–83. Two volumes. See text for this and others of Sandby's works

Scott, Sir Walter *Border Antiquities of England and Scotland*, London 1814–17. Two volumes, with 96 copper engraved plates by J. Greig, most of them after Luke Clennell

Stanfield, Clarkson *Coast Scenery*, London 1836. 40 plates all after Stanfield by the Findens, Miller, Brandard, Kernot and others, most of whom had worked for Turner. A very fine steel-engraved volume

Stark, James, and Robberds, J. W. *Scenery of the Rivers of Norfolk*, Norwich and London 1834. 35 plates after Stark, engraved by Miller, G. Cooke, Goodall, W. R. Smith, Kernot, Wallis, Forrest, W. Radclyffe and a few others. A very fine publication (see text) with some exceptionally good plates and vignettes

Stockdale, F. W. L. *Etchings from Original Antiquities in the County of Kent*, London 1811. 39 hand-coloured etchings

Storer, J. S. *The Antiquarian Itinerary*, London 1815–18. Seven volumes, with 336 engraved plates by and after James Sargant Storer

—— *History and Antiquities of the Cathedral Churches of Great Britain*, 1814–18.

Four volumes, with 252 plates

Storer, J. and Greig, J. *Antiquarian and Topographical Cabinet*, London, W. Clarke, 1807–11. Ten volumes, with 500 copper engraved plates by Storer and Greig

Stukeley, William *Itinerarium Curiosum . . .*, 1724. With 98 engraved views

Talt, A. F. and Butterworth, E. *Views on the Manchester and Leeds Railway*, London 1845. 20 tinted lithograph plates

Tillotson, J. *Beauties of English Scenery*, London, Allman, c1860. 36 steel-engraved plates after Bartlett, T. M. Baynes, Cox, G. Shepherd, Gastineau, W. Daniell, C. Radclyffe, Purser, by Adlard, Lacey, Rogers, J. C. Allen, Acon, J. Miller, Deeble, T. H. Shepherd, W. Radclyffe, H. Wallis

Tombleson, W. *Eighty Picturesque Views on the Thames and Medway*, London, Tombleson & Co, 1834 and London, Black & Armstrong, c1840. All steel-engraved plates, except one, after Tombleson by H. Winkles, Tingle, Varrall, R. Sands, W. Lacey, Le Petit, How, Carter, Bishop and others. All in decorative borders

Walker, John *The Itinerant*, London 1799. The first edition contains 176 engravings by Walker after Girtin, Harraden, Orme, Dayes, Varley, W. Turner, Nixon and others

Walpoole, G. A. *The New British Traveller*, London 1784. With maps and many copper engravings

Watts, W. *The Seats of the Nobility and Gentry*, London 1779. With 84 copper-engraved plates by Watts after Rooker, Sandby, Malton, Barrett and others

West, T. *A Guide to the Lakes*, London 1796. 16 tinted aquatints by S. Alken and others and 2 engravings by Byrne after Farington. The aquatint plates were issued separately as *Sixteen Views of the Lakes in Cumberland and Westmorland*, drawn by J. Smith and J. Emes and aquatinted by S. Alken

Westall, W. See under 'Painters' for his publications

Westall, W. and Moule, T. *Great Britain Illustrated*, London, Tilt, 1830. 118 steel-engraved plates on 59 sheets, all after Westall by E. Finden, E. Francis, J. Fife, S. Rawle, Roffe and Taylor. Divided into two volumes, *The Landscape Album*, 1st and 2nd series, 1832–4

Wright, T. and Jones, Revd H. L. *Memorials of Cambridge*, London, Oxford and Cambridge 1841–2. Two volumes with 74 steel-engraved plates by John Le Keux after J. A. Bell and F. Mackenzie, and 76 woodcuts

SCOTLAND

The prospects of various Scottish towns etched and engraved by John Slezer are among the most interesting and informative of early topographical prints.

The view of Edinburgh from the north, a plate nearly three feet in width, is a notable example. Edinburgh itself, Shepherd's 'Modern Athens', was the subject of a very large number of illustrations, including two series of fine lithographs by J. D. Harding and Samuel Swarbreck. Other attractive sites included the Falls of Clyde, Kelso Abbey—there is a particularly fine aquatint by F. Jukes after C. Catton and another by F. C. Lewis after W. Wilson—and the various locations made famous by the works of Burns and Scott. Among the islands, Staffa exerted a strong fascination and there are several lithographs of it; Ferguson's plate of Fingal's Cave after W. A. Nesfield is a good specimen. William Daniell used nine views of Staffa; his *Voyage around Great Britain* included 156 Scottish coastal views, among the very best of his aquatints.

A Catalogue of . . . 50,000 Prints and Drawings Illustrating the Topography and Antiquities of England and Wales, Scotland and Ireland, published in 1878, has 1,433 Scottish items, whereas a single English county, Norfolk, has 1,164. And Abbey's *Scenery* lists as many collections devoted to Brighton as to the whole of Scotland. Difficulty of access is the reason for the comparative scarcity of earlier Scottish views. Until the coming of the railways, north of Edinburgh was terra incognita to all but the most hardy and adventurous, and the memory of the '45 rebellion lasted a very long time.

Baynes, T. M. *Twenty Views of the City and Environs of Edinburgh*, London 1823. 20 lithographs by Baynes printed by Hullmandel

Beattie, W. *Scotland Illustrated in a Series of Views*, London 1838. Two volumes with 119 steel engravings, nearly all after Bartlett and Allom by Varrall, Fisher, Deeble, Adlard, J. Cousen, Sands, W. Radclyffe and others. Later extended as *Caledonia Illustrated* with 167 plates

Billings, Robert William *The Baronial and Ecclesiastical Antiquities of Scotland*, Edinburgh and London 1845–52. Four volumes, each with 60 engravings after Billings by G. B. Smith, J. H. Le Keux, J. Godfrey, J. Redaway, J. Saddler, and G. Winter

Browne, J. *A History of the Highlands*, Edinburgh and London c1875. Four volumes, with 25 engraved views and portraits, tartans etc. Views after J. C. Brown, Fleming, Mackenzie, Donaldson engraved by Swan, Forrest, J. Smith and others

Forsyth, R. *The Beauties of Scotland*, Edinburgh 1805–8. Five volumes, with over one hundred copper-engraved plates

Fullarton & Co *A Series of Select Views in Perthshire*, London, Edinburgh and Dublin 1844. With 79 steel engravings

Garnett, T. *Observations on a Tour through the Highlands and Part of the Western Isles of Scotland*, London 1800. Two volumes, with 51 tinted aquatints by

W. H. Watts

Hill, D. O. *The Land of Burns*, Glasgow, Edinburgh and London 1840. Two volumes, with 77 engravings after Hill by Miller, Richardson, Forrest, Woolnoth, Robinson and others

Lawson, John Parker *Scotland Delineated*, London 1847-54. Contains 71 tinted lithographs printed by Day & Son. The artists include David Roberts, Cattermole, Clarkson Stanfield, J. M. W. Turner, W. L. Leitch, Joseph Nash and J. D. Harding, who himself did most of the lithographic drawing. One of the major British lithographic publications

Leighton, John *Select Views of Glasgow and its Environs*, Glasgow 1828. With 33 plates engraved by Joseph Swan, who also published the collection

— — *The Lakes of Scotland*, Glasgow 1834, and Edinburgh and London 1839. 49 steel engravings by Joseph Swan after John Fleming

Maitland, William *The History of Edinburgh*, Edinburgh 1753. With 20 copper-engraved plates by Fourdrinier

Nattes, John Claude, and Fittler, James *Scotia Depicta*, London 1819. Originally published in parts, 1804. Contains 48 etched plates by Fittler after Nattes

Robson, George Fennel *Scenery of the Grampian Mountains*, London 1814. With 41 soft-ground etchings by Henry Morton after Robson. A coloured issue was also published, 1819, with the plates aquatinted in tones of brown and purple

Schetky, John C. and Heath, James *Illustrations of Walter Scott's Lay of the Last Minstrel*, London 1808. 12 engraved plates of river scenes by Heath after Schetky, and two vignettes

Scott, Sir Walter *Provincial Antiquities and Picturesque Scenery of Scotland*, London and Edinburgh 1826. Two volumes, with 50 engravings after Turner, Thomson, Blore, Calcott, Schetky and Nasmyth by Goodall, H. Le Keux, G. Cooke, Woolnoth, Hollis, W. R. Smith, Miller, Allen, Sands and W. Cooke

Shepherd, Thomas Hosmer *Modern Athens!*, London 1829. With 101 steel engravings after Shepherd by Tombleson, Lacey, Watkins, Bond, Lizars, Radclyffe, T. Barber, Henshall, Acon, Hinchcliffe, J. B. Allen, Cruse, Higham, Fox and others

Slezer, John *Theatrum Scotiae*, London 1693. Contains 57 etched and engraved plates, some by and after the Dutchman Johannes van den Aveele and some engraved by Robert White. It is said to be the first book containing town prospects published in Britain

Stoddart, John *Remarks on Local Scenery and Manners in Scotland During the Years 1799 and 1800*, London. Two volumes, with 32 coloured aquatints by Nattes, Merigot and others. Also published uncoloured and found more frequently thus

Storer, J. and H. S. *Views in Edinburgh and its Vicinity*, Edinburgh 1820. Two volumes, with 97 copper-engraved plates

Storer, J. and Greig, J. *Views in North Britain, Illustrative of the Works of Robert Burns*, London 1805. With 18 copper-engraved plates

Sutherland, Duchess of *Views in Orkney and on the North-Eastern Coast of Scotland*, privately printed 1807. 120 copies only. With 43 etchings by Her Ladyship

Swarbreck, S. D. *Sketches in Scotland*, London 1839. 24 plates drawn and lithographed by Swarbreck

— — *Views of Edinburgh*, London 1839. A collection of coloured views drawn and lithographed by Swarbreck, comparable with T. S. Boys' *London As It Is*

Tillotson, J. *Album of Scottish Scenery*, London 1860. 26 plates after Stanfield, Copley Fielding, Robson, Harding, W. Westall, Turner, Roberts, Cattermole and others engraved by the Findens, Fisher, W. Radclyffe, W. R. Smith, W. B. Cooke, Adlard, Simmons and others. The scenes illustrate places in Scott's works

— —*The New Waverley Album*, London 1859. 25 plates engraved by E. Finden after Stanfield, Roberts, W. Daniell, Copley Fielding, Cattermole, Prout, de Wint, W. Westall, Barret, Nash and S. Austin

Turner de Lond, W. *Scotia Delineata*, Edinburgh *c*1825. 4 lithograph plates, hand-coloured. The same artist (whoever he may have been) produced 2 lithographs of the Great Fire in Edinburgh, 1824, also hand-coloured. These are plates of particular quality

Wilson, John *Scotland Illustrated in a Series of Eighty Views*, 80 steel engravings after drawings by John C. Brown, William Brown, John Fleming, W. B. Scott and other Scottish artists

WALES

One of the earliest engravings of a Welsh view is Kip's Chepstow Castle, published in *Britannia Illustrata* and in Atkyns' *Glostershire*. It is also one of Kip's most successful compositions. The Buck brothers published three volumes of Welsh views between 1740 and 1742 and also included Wrexham, Cardiff and Swansea in their prospects of towns. Another interesting early Welsh print is W. H. Toms' etching and engraving of Hawarden Castle and Park in Flintshire, after a bird's-eye drawing by Thomas Badeslade. Toms' pupil, John Boydell, included several Welsh castles in his engravings.

Richard Wilson painted many Welsh scenes; Edward Rooker, with his son Michael, engraved 'The Summit of Cader-Idris Mountain' after Wilson's

Academy exhibit about 1775. Sandby's series of aquatints were issued at this time. Another major set of Welsh aquatints was the illustrations of Hafod, by Stadler after John 'Warwick' Smith.

Illustrated Welsh tours include Wyndham's and Pennant's, Gilpin's *Wye* and Ireland's *Wye*, Coxe's *Monmouthshire* and Pugh's *Cambria Depicta*. Of the steel-engraved collections, Gastineau's and Roscoe's are the chief examples. Wood's *Rivers of Wales* contains a notable set of etchings, while among the better lithographs are those by George Hawkins of the bridges at Conway and across the Menai Straits. Daniell's aquatints, which first appeared in the early numbers of the *Voyage around Great Britain*, are the pre-eminent coastal views.

The National Museum of Wales' catalogue of Welsh Topographical Prints (1926), listing all its prints from 1730 to 1850, produces the following top ten:

1 Caernarvon Castle (88)
2 Tintern Abbey (79)
3 Conway Castle (69)
4 Chepstow (68)
5 Llandaff Cathedral and Bishop's Palace (50)
6 St David's Cathedral and Bishop's Palace (42)
7 Cardiff Castle (37)
   Raglan Castle (37)
9 Cardiff and surrounding area (33)
10 Snowdon (31)

In the *Catalogue of 50,000 Prints and Drawings*, 1878, a total of 1,242 Welsh prints is found. This includes forty-two views of Tintern Abbey, drawn and/or engraved by the following: Lacey, Smith, Grey, Bartlett, Harraden, Grose, Fielding, Ireland, the Bucks, Haghe, Harwood, Havell, Le Keux, Taylor, Coney, Buckler, Horner, Beeks, Willes, Godfrey, Sharpe, Byrne, Needham, Harris and Cooper; thirty more were anonymous. Nearly all these were copper engravings.

Batty, Capt R. *Welsh Scenery*, London 1823. Contains 35 steel engravings by Edward Finden after Batty's drawings

Broughton, B. *Six Picturesque Views in North Wales*, London 1801. Includes 6 aquatints by S. Alken after Broughton. An earlier edition (1798) had 4 plates only

Clark, Edwin *The Britannia and Conway Tubular Bridges*, London 1850. Two volumes of text, including 18 lithographs, and one volume of plates, with 6 tinted lithographs and 40 others. The tinted lithographs are by George Hawkins

Coxe, William *An Historical Tour in Monmouthshire*, London 1801. Includes 55 engraved views after Sir Robert Hoare, engraved by W. Byrne

Dibdin, T. C. *The Waterfalls of Carnarvonshire*, London, Dickinson, c1845. 6 tinted lithographs

Fielding, Anthony Vandyke Copley *Illustrations of the River Wye*, London 1821. With 28 aquatints by T. H. Fielding

Freeman, G. J. *Sketches in Wales*, London 1826. With 15 lithographs by T. M. Baynes printed by Hullmandel

Gastineau, Henry *Wales Illustrated*, London, Jones & Co, 1830

—— *South Wales Illustrated*, London, Jones & Co, 1830. 224 steel engravings by Mottram, W. Wallis, W. Radclyffe, Adlard, J. B. Allen, Varrall, Lacey, Higham, Barber, Deeble, Acon, Bond, Tingle and others. A very large number of Welsh prints come from this source

Gilpin, William *Observations on the River Wye*, London 1782. With 16 oval tinted aquatints after Gilpin

Hoare, Sir Richard Colt *A Collection of Forty-Eight Views . . . in North and South Wales*, London, Boydell, c1806. Most of the drawings are by Hoare, engraved by Basire, Byrne, Watts and others

Ireland, Samuel *Picturesque Views on the River Wye*, London 1797. 31 sepia aquatints after Ireland, by C. Apostool

Jones, Henry Longueville *Illustrations of the Natural Scenery of the Snowdonian Mountains*, London 1829. With 15 lithographs printed by Hullmandel

Malkin, Benjamin Heath *The Scenery, Antiquities and Biography of South Wales*, London 1804. With 12 plates, tinted in various colours, drawn and engraved by Laporte

Newell, R. H. *Letters on the Scenery of South Wales*, London 1821. With 5 aquatints by T. Sutherland and 15 tinted etchings, after Newell. Also published with coloured aquatints

Norris, Charles *Etchings of Tenby*, London 1812. 38 etched plates by Norris, mostly of buildings

Pennant, Thomas *Tours in Wales*, London 1810. Three volumes, with 43 copper-engraved plates after Moses Griffith

Pugh, Edward *Cambria Depicta: A Tour through North Wales*, London 1816. With 70 coloured aquatints by 'a native artist'

Roscoe, Thomas *Wanderings and Excursions in North Wales*, 1836. 51 good steel engravings by W. Radclyffe after David Cox, Creswick, Cattermole, Wrightson and Watson

—— *Wanderings and Excursions in South Wales, including the Scenery of the River Wye*. 48 steel engravings by W. Radclyffe after the same painters as above, plus Copley Fielding, the younger D. Cox and a couple more. (These engravings have been described as 'the pinnacle of achievement in the field of engraved topographical work')

Smith, J. E. *Fifteen Views Illustrative of a Tour to Hafod, in Cardiganshire, the seat of Thomas Johnes, MP*, London, White & Co, 1810. 15 sepia aquatints by J. C. Stadler after originals by John 'Warwick' Smith. Sir James Edward Smith wrote the original text, but the plates were also issued on their own

Tillotson, J. *Picturesque Scenery in Wales*, London 1860. 37 steel engravings, mostly from Gastineau's previous publications

Williams, David *The History of Monmouthshire*, London and Monmouth 1796. With 36 aquatints by J. Gardnor and J. Hill. There were apparently 32 coloured aquatint copies published as well

Wood, J. G. *Six Views in the Neighbourhood of Llangollen and Bala*. Aquatints by Maria Catherine Prestel, using two different tints of ink. Dedicated to Lady Eleanor Butler and Miss Ponsonby, the 'Ladies of Llangollen'

—— *The Principal Rivers of Wales Illustrated*, London, Bensley, 1813. Two volumes, with 157 tinted etched plates, fine, delicate and rare

Wyndham, Henry Penruddocke *A Tour through Monmouthshire and Wales*, Salisbury 1781. 15 engravings after Samuel Heironymous Grimm

PAINTERS AND DRAUGHTSMEN

This list gives brief details of many, though by no means all, of the artists whose work was reproduced by one of the methods under discussion during the period covered by this Guide. Most of the engravings appeared in periodicals and bound volumes; some were issued as single prints or in small sets. The number of paintings each artist exhibited in the major London galleries—The Royal Academy, the Old Water Colour Society (OWCS), the British Institution and so forth—is given, but provincial exhibitions are excluded. The painters themselves range from the giants of the age—Turner, Constable—to the run-of-the-mill illustrators, of whom W. H. Bartlett and Thomas Allom are chief examples. What they have in common is that they painted places rather than people or still life and that their work was made known to a wide public through one of the reproductive processes.

PAINTERS

Allom, Thomas (1804–72) Landscape and architectural subjects; exhibited 60 paintings. Widely travelled. Did most of the drawings for *Lake and Mountain Scenery*, *c*1830, and *The British Switzerland*, two volumes, 1858, as well as several volumes of views overseas. A competent painter, his work shows evidence of his architectural training

Balmer, George (1806–46) Mostly known as a marine and coastal painter. 47 works exhibited. Painted several of the north-east coast scenes for Finden's *Ports and Harbours*

Barker, Benjamin (1776–1838) One of the Bath family. His *Landscape Scenery near Bath*, aquatinted by T. H. Fielding, 48 plates, was published 1824. Exhibited 246 paintings in all. Brother of T. Barker, one of the earliest English artists to try lithography

Barnard, George (*fl c*1832–84) Teacher and illustrator, who exhibited 95 paintings. *Richmond and its surrounding Scenery*, by W. B. Cooke, is after his drawings

Bartlett, William Henry (1809–54) One of the most prolific of illustrators for topographical works. Exhibited only 6 paintings but his work appeared in —among other publications—Barber's *Isle of Wight*, Beattie's *Castles and Abbeys of England* (all the plates) and *Scotland Illustrated*, Britton & Brayley's *Devonshire and Cornwall Illustrated*, Finden's *Ports and Harbours*, Moore's *History of Devonshire*, Shepherd's *Bath and Bristol*, Woodward's *Winchester* and *Hampshire*, Wright's *Essex* and several volumes of continental and Irish views. He even got one plate into the Nattali publication of Turner's so-called *Antiquarian and Picturesque Tour round the South Coast*. It is almost certain that there are more steel engravings after Bartlett than after any other painter of views

Baynes, Thomas Mann (1794–*c*1852) Exhibited 51 paintings. A few plates after him in Tillotson's *Beauties of English Scenery* and Wright & Allen's *Lancashire*. Freeman's *Sketches in Wales* has 15 plates drawn on stone by him. Several views also in Moore's *Devonshire*

Bourne, James (1773–1854) Topographical painter whose drawings were engraved in various publications

Bourne, John Cooke (1814–96) See text

Boys, Thomas Shotter (1803–74) See text. Exhibited 174 paintings, his best work being town views

Brandard, Robert (1805–62) See under engravers. Exhibited 66 paintings

Buckler, John (1770–1851) and **Buckler, John Chessel** (1793–1894), his son. Work very similar. Whitaker's *History of Richmondshire* contained some of J. Buckler's work, along with Turner's

Cattermole, George (1800–68) Worked for John Britton. Exhibited 105 paintings. Roscoe's *North Wales*, Rutter's *Fonthill Abbey*, Black's *Picturesque Tourist of Scotland*, Tillotson's *Waverley Album* contain examples of his work

Clennell, Luke (1781–1840) One of Bewick's most notable apprentices. Wood engraver, then painter, exhibiting 70 works. Provided most of the drawings for Scott's *Border Antiquities*, engraved by Greig, and several vignettes for Turner's *Southern Coast*. Became insane *c*1817 and never fully recovered. An artist of quality

Constable, John (1776–1837) See text for mezzotints of his work by David Lucas

Cooke, Edward William (1811–80) Son of G. Cooke, engraver. Exhibited

256 paintings. Marine and coastal painter, see Finden's *Ports and Harbours*. Also etcher of much distinction: *Shipping and Craft*, 1829

Cotman, John Sell (1782–1842) See text

Cox, David (1783–1859) Exhibited 973 paintings. Pupil of J. Varley, a drawing-master and one of the greatest watercolourists. Much of his work engraved by W. Radclyffe for Roscoe's *Grand Junction Railway*, *North* and *South Wales* and Twamley's *Annual of British Landscape Scenery; an Autumn Ramble on the Wye.* Cox and Radclyffe made a brilliant partnership, one of the best in steel-engraved reproduction

Creswick, Thomas (1811–69) 266 paintings exhibited, most of them at the RA, which indicates his preference for oils. Finden's *Ports and Harbours*, Redding's itineraries of Cornwall and Lancaster, Ritchie's *Wye*, and Roscoe's *North* and *South Wales* are among books in which his work appears

Cristall, Joshua (1767–1847) Exhibited 382 paintings, almost all high-quality watercolours, of which surprisingly few were engraved

Crome, John (1768–1821) See text

Daniell, William (1769–1837) Exhibited 232 paintings, the majority at the RA. Engraved his own watercolour landscapes for his *Voyage around Great Britain* and other series of views. See text

Dayes, Edward (1763–1804) One of the leading early watercolourists. 12 plates copper engraved for his *Picturesque Tour through … Derbyshire and Yorkshire*, 1805; E. W. Brayley collected this and other works and published them for the benefit of his widow after he committed suicide. Girtin was a pupil of his

Delamotte, William (1775–1863) Exhibited 84 paintings. His *Colleges, Chapels and Gardens of Oxford*, 25 plates, lithographed by W. Gauci, appeared in 1842. Also published *30 Etchings of Rural Subjects*, 1816, and illustrations of Virginia Water

De Loutherbourg, Philip James (1740–1812) Born Strasbourg; came to England and was much involved with scene-painting and theatre generally. Exhibited 155 paintings, most of them at the RA. *Picturesque Scenery of Great Britain*, 6 plates, 1801, coloured aquatints by Stadler, re-engraved 1806 by J. Hill, were followed by *Romantic and Picturesque Scenery of England and Wales*, 18 plates, engraved by W. Pickett and coloured by John Clark. In some of his paintings we see the summit of Romanticism

De Wint, Peter (1784–1849) One of the greatest watercolourists, exhibiting 454 paintings, nearly all at the OWCS. Several plates after him in *Picturesque Views in London*, engraved by Charles Heath, 1825; a few in Tillotson's publications and a couple in Turner's *Southern Coast*

Dodgson, George Haydock (1811–80) Exhibited 414 paintings. Engravings after his railway scenery appeared in Roscoe's *Grand Junction Railway* and *London and Birmingham Railway* and in *Illustrations of the Scenery on the Line of the Whitby and Pickering Railway*, 1836

Duncan, Edward (1803–82) Best known as a marine artist, with 558 exhibits, mostly watercolour. Very little of his topographical work seems to have been used in books: one plate in Finden's *Ports and Harbours* and one in Roscoe's *London and Birmingham Railway*

Farington, Joseph (1747–1821) Probably best known for his diary, first two volumes of which were published in full 1978. Exhibited 110 paintings. Stadler's aquatints for Boydell's *Thames* (text by William Combe) are after his paintings. His Lake scenes were engraved by Byrne, Medland, Pouncy and others and published 1816. Rebecca West has commented, not unkindly, that his views were as if seen by a sheep

Fielding, Anthony Vandyke Copley (1787–1855) Exhibited 1,789 pictures, mostly watercolours. His *Illustrations of the River Wye*, 1821, has 28 plates engraved in aquatint by T. H. Fielding; there was a poorer edition of 12 plates in 1841. Plates after him are also in Roscoe's *North* and *South Wales*, Tillotson's *Scottish Scenery* and *Waverley Album* and Wright's *Lancashire*

Fielding, Theodore Henry Adolphus (1781–1851) Eldest son of Theodore Nathan. Wrote *Art of Engraving*, 1841, and other books on painting. *Cumberland, Westmorland and Lancashire Illustrated*, 1822, has 44 coloured aquatints after him; *Picturesque Tour of the English Lakes*, 1821, has 48 plates after him with J. Walton (issued in twelve monthly parts for £3 13s 6d complete, or six guineas in large size)

Francia, François Louis Thomas (1772–1839) He taught Bonington and worked with Girtin; exhibited 201 paintings. Two vignettes of his are in Turner's *Southern Coast*

Gainsborough, Thomas (1727–88) See text

Gardnor, Revd John (1729–1808) Exhibited 88 paintings, mostly at the RA. Many of the aquatint plates in William David's *History of Monmouthshire*, 1796, are after his originals. According to Abbey, only 32 coloured copies of this book were issued; there was a much larger issue with uncoloured plates. He was an artist before becoming vicar of Battersea

Gastineau, Henry (c1791–1876) Very prolific 'picturesque' landscape painter, with 1,341 exhibits, almost all at the OWCS. *Wales Illustrated*, 1830, contains 224 plates engraved by Deeble, Lacey, Varrall, Wallis and others, all after his drawings. His work was also reproduced in various Scottish and Northern England sets of views. He was a drawing-master. Much of his own work was influenced by Turner; he shows some style and compositional skill

Geikie, Walter (1795–1837) Scottish landscape painter who was deaf and dumb. Two views in Dibdin's *Northern Tour*; also a collection of etchings, 1841

Gendall, John (1790–1865) Worked for Ackermann. Contributed drawings to *Views of Country Seats*, 1823–8, with Westall and Shepherd, aquatinted by T. Sutherland

Gilpin, Revd William (1724–1804) Never an exhibitor. See text

Girtin, Thomas (1775–1802) Apprenticed to Dayes and employed as print colourer by J. R. Smith. Brilliant watercolourist. A few engravings after him in *Copper Plate Magazine*, 1792 et seq. May have worked over James Moore's sketches for *Views in the Southern Part of Scotland*, aquatints, 1792. Excellent etchings of Paris, 1802

Green, William (1761–1823) Lake District painter and engraver. He published engravings after his own drawings in 1808, 1809, 1810 and 1814; his *Series of Sixty Small Prints* contained 60 soft-ground etchings of Lake District views, published by himself at Ambleside

Griffith, Moses (1747–1819) Mainly self-taught as a draughtsman, he became Thomas Pennant's servant, accompanying him on his tours and making many drawings for his books. His designs are adequate but not outstanding

Grose, Francis (1731–91) Amateur artist. Antiquarian, among his publications were *Antiquities of England and Wales*, 1773–87, and *Antiquarian Repository*, 1775. He was a rather portly military gentleman. Redgrave notes that he was 'the chiel amang ye taking notes', of whom Burns wrote:

> Now by the powers o' verse and prose,
> Thou art a dainty chiel, O Grose!

This was presumably before he put on weight.

Hakewill, James (1778–1843) Architect and draughtsman. Published several architectural works, including *Windsor and its Neighbourhood*, 1813, with his own drawings and plans

Harding, James Duffield (1797–1863) Exhibited 208 paintings, his first when aged 13. Taught by Samuel Prout and the engraver James Pye. His work is in Finden's *Ports and Harbours*, Ritchie's *Windsor Castle and its Environs*, 1840, and a few other volumes. He was one of the major lithographers, with three of his own collections—*The Park and the Forest*, 1841, was especially fine—and much work for Hullmandel. He was a teacher, Ruskin being one of his pupils. Many of his paintings are of foreign scenes. A fine and interesting artist

Harraden, Richard (1756–1838) Working with his son, R.B., he published *Cantabrigia Depicta*, 1809, with 34 engravings. R.B. drew *Illustrations of the University of Cambridge*, 1830

Hassell, John (1767–1825) Exhibited 21 paintings. Friend and biographer of George Morland. Drawing-master, publishing *Art of Drawing in Water Colours*, and *Aqua Pictura*, 1813, and many coloured aquatint volumes after his own drawings. His *Tour of the Isle of Wight*, 1790, has 30 tinted oval aquatints of little merit. This was followed by *Picturesque Guide to Bath*, etc (with Ibbetson and Laporte), 1792, *Picturesque Rides and Walks . . . round the British Metropolis*, 1817, with 120 plates, some engraved by Havell, *Tour of the Grand Junction Canal, Noblemen's and Gentlemen's Seats* and *Pleasure and Sport on the Thames*, 1823. On the whole his later work is the better

Havell, William (1782–1857) The most prolific painter of the large family of Havells, exhibiting 331 works. His *Series of Picturesque Views of the River Thames*, 1812, with 12 coloured aquatints engraved by his brothers Robert and Daniel, is the nearest rival to Westall and·Owen's *Thames*. His Hastings view is in Turner's *Southern Coast* and he contributed 6 drawings to Robert Havell's engravings of *Noblemen's and Gentlemen's Seats*. An important water-colour painter, less impressive in oils

Hearne, Thomas (1744–1817) Apprenticed to Woollett. Began as engraver; then concentrated on drawing and produced *Antiquities of Great Britain*, 1777–86, engraved by William Byrne, Middiman and others. Also made drawings for *Britannia Depicta*, 1806–18. A noted watercolourist, especially good on trees and skies; he controlled his work in the interests of the engravers. Exhibited 78 paintings

Hofland, Thomas Christopher (1777–1843) A drawing-master. Employed by George III for a time, and by the Duke of Marlborough for whom he painted views of White Knights for engraving. His drawings were in E. Rhodes' *Yorkshire Scenery*, 1826, and his own *British Anglers' Manual*, 1839, with 14 plates, of which 10 are views, engraved by W. R. Smith. He exhibited 339 pictures. 'His art was peculiar', said Redgrave. 'His aim was to convey poetical impressions, but he never rose to the front rank, probably kept back by the many struggles and difficulties he had to encounter'

Holland, Peter Exhibited in Liverpool from 1787. His *Select Views of the Lakes*, 1792, has 21 aquatints by C. Rosenberg

Ibbetson, Julius Caesar (1759–1817) A scene painter who moved on to oils and watercolours, with 87 exhibits. Contributed to *Picturesque Guide to Bath*, etc, with Hassell and Laporte, 1792. Also illustrated *Cabinet of Quadrupeds* and wrote *An Accidence or Gamut of painting in Watercolours*

Jewitt, Arthur (1772–1852) Topographical writer and painter. Publications include *History of Lancashire*, 1810, *History of Buxton*, 1811, and *Matlock Companion*, 1835

Kirby, John Joshua (1716–74) Friend of Gainsborough. Made 12 drawings for *Monasteries, Castles, etc in Suffolk*, 1748, which he etched himself, followed by others engraved by J. Wood. Woollett engraved his views of Kew

Laporte, John (1761–1839) Exhibited 289 paintings. Some plates in Hutchins' *History of Dorset* after him. Also worked with Wells on etchings after Gainsborough, and contributed the plates to Malkin's *South Wales*

Leitch, William Leighton (1804–83) Exhibited 220 paintings. Some engravings by Kernot, Willmore, W. B. Cooke and Bradshaw after his pictures appeared in Adams' *Isle of Wight*, 1856

Lewis, Frederic Christian (1779–1856) Exhibited 160 paintings. A good etcher and an excellent aquatint engraver, he published several collections of etchings and aquatints after his own paintings of the Dart, Exe, Tamar and Tavy. His *Scenery of the Devonshire Rivers*, 1843, all his work, is a fine collection

Mackenzie, Frederick (1787–1854) Exhibited 115 paintings, mainly of buildings. He made several drawings for the *Beauties*, *Architectural Antiquities* and *Cathedral Antiquities* of John Britton, 34 drawings for Ackermann's *Westminster*, and some for his *Oxford* and *Cambridge*. The hundred plates engraved by John Le Keux for Ingram's *Memorials of Oxford*, 1837, are after his drawings; most of Le Keux's engravings in *Memorials of Cambridge*, 1841, are also after him, the rest being after J. A. Bell. He contributed several drawings to Charles Heath's *Views in London*, 1825, to Rickman's *Styles of Architecture* and Todd's *History of the College of Bonhommes*, 1823. A master of perspective and accurate drawing

Malton, Thomas jnr (1748–1817) Expert architectural illustrator, with 130 paintings exhibited. Taught perspective; Turner was a pupil of his. *Picturesque Tour through the Cities of London and Westminster*, 1792, contains 100 of his drawings aquatinted by himself. His *Picturesque Views of the City of Oxford* was published 1802. Buildings were his chief preoccupation

Marlow, William (1740–1813) Exhibited 152 pictures, including many Thames views, some of which have been copper engraved

Marshall, Charles (1806–90) Exhibited 312 paintings. Scene painter and landscape artist. Most of the plates in Henshall's *Select Illustrated Topography of Thirty Miles round London*, 1839, text by W. E. Trotter, are after him, engraved by the Henshalls, Floyd, Bentley and Varrall

Nash, Frederick (1782–1856) Exhibited 616 paintings. Student of Thomas Malton jnr and an expert architectural draughtsman. Many of his drawings used in Britton's and Ackermann's publications. Held in high esteem by Turner

Nattes, John Claude (c1765–1822) Exhibited 84 paintings but dismissed from the OWCS for showing other painters' works in his own name. Some plates in *Oxford Delineated*, 1805, are after him

Neale, John Preston (1771–1847) Started as a post office clerk and became a watercolourist of some note, with 74 exhibits (oils among them). Made the drawings for *History and Antiquities of the Abbey Church at Westminster*, 1818–23, two series of *Seats of the Nobility and Gentry*, 1822–4 and 1829, *Graphic Illustrations of Fonthill Abbey*, 1824 (5 of the 6 plates), *An Account of the Deep-Dene in Surrey*, 1826, and contributed a few drawings for Shepherd's *Bath and Bristol*, 1829

Nicholson, Francis (1753–1844) Exhibited 318 paintings, mostly watercolours. 14 plates after his drawings published in the *Copper Plate Magazine*, 1792–1801. Romantic in style. Also a lithographer

Nixon, John (c1750–1818). An amateur painter, who also etched. He made some drawings for Pennant's *London to the Isle of Wight*

Noble, William Bonneau (1780–1831) Exhibited few paintings but drew for *Guide to Watering Places on the Coast*, 1817, 15 plates

Owen, Samuel (1768–1857) Mainly known as a marine painter, with 37 exhibits. Two vignettes in Turner's *Southern Coast*, but best known for his five splendid plates, aquatinted by Reeve, in *Picturesque Tour of the Thames*, 1828. W. Westall drew the non-tidal views; as a marine expert, Owen did the others

Payne, William (c1760–1830) Drawing-master, much admired in his day. Exhibited 108 paintings, many West Country views. Engravings after him in Middiman's *Select Views*; he also issued a set of etchings, *Six Views near Plymouth*, c1810, after his own drawings. His *Picturesque Views in Devonshire, Cornwall*, etc, 16 plates, collected 1826, were aquatinted in colour by W. Pickett and others. Also *Picturesque Description of North Wales*, collected 1823, with 20 plates

Pickering, George (1794–1857) Well known for his lithographs, he also provided drawings for Ormerod's *History of Cheshire* and Baines' *Lancashire*

Prout, Samuel (1783–1852) A Devonshire painter, with 656 exhibits and a high reputation as a teacher. Contributed to *The Antiquarian and Topographical Cabinet*, 1805–11, Britton and Brayley's *Beauties, Relics of Antiquity*, 1810–12, *Picturesque Delineations in Devon and Cornwall, Studies of Cottages and Rural*

Scenery, 1816 (the last 2 contain soft-ground etchings by him after his own drawings). Also a few aquatints after his own drawings and a couple of vignettes in *Southern Coast*

Pyne, William Henry (1769–1843) Exhibited 232 landscapes and coastal scenes. Art journalist and historian. Etched several hundred figure groups for his *Microcosm*, aquatinted by J. Hill, *c*1806

Pugin, Augustus Charles (1762–1832) Worked for many of Ackermann's publications (*Microcosm*, *Oxford*, *Cambridge* among them), contributing drawings of buildings to which Rowlandson added the figures. Father of A. W. N. Pugin, the Gothic revivalist

Radclyffe, Charles Walter (1817–87) Exhibited 34 paintings and provided drawings for several topographical works including Roscoe's *Grand Junction* and *London and Birmingham* railway books

Richardson, Thomas Miles (1784–1848) A Newcastle painter, exhibiting 90 pictures in London. His son of the same name worked similarly, hence attribution is difficult at times. Several plates after Richardson in T. F. Dibdin's *Bibliographical and Antiquarian and Picturesque Tour in the Northern Counties*, 1838

Robertson, George (1724–88) Exhibited 87 paintings. The six well-known Coalbrookdale engravings are after his originals

Robson, George Fennel (1788–1833) Exhibited 700 paintings, mostly watercolours. His *Scenery of the Grampian Mountains* has 41 plates, engraved by H. Morton, 1819. Made the 31 drawings for Britton's publication *Picturesque Views of the English Cities*, 1828

Rooker, Michael 'Angelo' (1743–1801) Scene painter and engraver; his father Edward was also an engraver. Drew and engraved several scenes for Oxford Almanacks. Best with buildings; much of his work was engraved by others in various collections of copper engravings

Rowlandson, Thomas (1756–1827) Contributed figures to drawings by Pugin for many of Ackermann's coloured books. His Dr Syntax etchings, to Combe's text, satirised the picturesque fashion. An important and delightful artist, but not a topographer in any significant sense. *Excursions to Brighton*, 1790, contained 8 sepia aquatints after his drawings, and there are 12 plates (coloured aquatints) after him in *Oxford and Cambridge*, 1809–11

Sandby, Paul and Thomas. See text

Schnebbelie, Jacob (1760–92) Antiquarian draughtsman, his work appearing in *Vetusta Monumenta* and *Monastic Remains and Ancient Castles*, 1791–2. Jukes aquatinted his view of the Serpentine, 1786

Shepherd, George (*c*1760–*c*1831) Some of his drawings were engraved in

Wilkinson's *Londina Illustrata*, and Pennant's *London* may carry a few in extra-illustrated editions. Worked with his son T. H. Shepherd on London aquatints for Ackermann's *Repository*

Shepherd, George Sidney (1801–61) Brother of T. H. Shepherd. Exhibited 283 paintings. Engravings after his drawings published in Mudie's *Hampshire*. Also drew for a series of lithographs, 1851, described as 'uninspired'

Shepherd, Thomas Hosmer (1793–1864) He made over 1,500 drawings of London, for the *Repository* (some reappearing in Papworth's *Select Views of London*, 1816), *London and its Environs* and *Metropolitan Improvements*. Also did work for Jones' *Bath and Bristol* and *Modern Athens*. See text

Smith, John 'Warwick' (1749–1831) Exhibited 162 paintings. Drew for Earl of Warwick. Middiman's *Select Views* has 6 engravings after him, and S. Alken aquatinted some of his drawings for Sotheby's *Tour through Parts of Wales*, 1794

Stanfield, Clarkson (1793–1867) Exhibited 178 paintings, mostly oils at the RA. Ex-navy, scene painter, marine expert. His *Coast Scenery* is one of the major collections of steel-engraved work. Heath's *Picturesque Annual*, 1832–4, also includes some of his drawings

Stark, James (1794–1859) Exhibited 274 paintings. See text for his *Rivers of Norfolk*

Stockdale, Frederick W. L. (c1790–1848) Exhibited 22 paintings. Worked for J. Britton and published etchings of Kent and Cornwall

Tomkins, Charles (1757–1823) An engraver and draughtsman. *Reading Abbey*, 1791, and the *Isle of Wight*, 1796, were illustrated after his drawings

Turner, Joseph Mallord William (1775–1851). See text

Varley, Cornelius (1781–1873) Exhibited 129 paintings. Some of his work was engraved for various publications, and he published a set of etchings of *Boats and other Craft on the Thames*

Varley, John (1778–1842) Exhibited 786 paintings, nearly all at the OWCS. Well known as a teacher. Some of his drawings copper engraved

Warren, Henry (1794–1879) Exhibited 263 paintings. Teacher and topographical illustrator. His work was engraved for Baines' *Lancashire* and *Yorkshire*, Finden's *Ports and Harbours*, and Roscoe's *South Wales*

Watson, Edward (*fl* 1830–50) Several engravings after his drawings are in Roscoe's *South Wales*

Westall, William (1781–1850) Exhibited 145 paintings. Younger brother of Richard. Draughtsman for foreign expeditions. Among the most frequently reproduced of artists, often aquatinting or lithographing his own drawings. Publications include *Views of Caves near Ingleton, Gordale Scar and Malham Cove*, 1818, *Abbeys and Castles in Yorkshire*, 1820, *Views in the Lakes*, 1820, *Picturesque Tour on the Thames* (with S. Owen), 1828, *Fountains Abbey and Studley Royal*, 1846 (these are aquatints). Lithographs include views of the Lakes, Edinburgh, the Thames and Windsor Castle. *Great Britain Illustrated* is a major collection of steel engravings after his drawings, also published as *The Landscape Album* in two volumes

Whittock, Nathaniel (*fl* 1828–48) Not an exhibitor, but his drawings were frequently reproduced, for example in T. Allen's *History of Surrey and Sussex*, 1829–30. *The Modern Picture of London, Westminster and the Metropolitan Boroughs*, c1836, contains 92 drawings all by him, and there are over 100 in Allen's *York*

Wild, Charles (1781–1835) Exhibited 178 paintings. Architectural specialist, mainly cathedrals and churches. Volumes including his work are *Canterbury*, 1807, *York*, 1808, *Chester*, 1813, *Lichfield*, 1813, *Lincoln*, 1819, *Worcester*, 1823; he also made 59 drawings for Pyne's *History of the Royal Residences*. Illustrated many foreign cathedrals. Went blind 1827

ENGRAVERS, ETCHERS AND LITHOGRAPHERS

This list names 275 of the engravers, etchers and lithographers working during our period. All those listed worked from topographical, or landscape, originals, hence many well-known names are absent—the mezzotinters of portraits, for example—because they fall outside the terms of reference. Again, this list makes no claim to be complete. It includes, I hope, the leaders of each particular craft, but to name all those at work during the period would mean producing a volume rather like a telephone directory. The absence of the name of the engraver of your favourite print means simply that there is not room to list everyone.

The etchers have recently been quite thoroughly researched, and Kenneth Guichard's *British Etchers 1850–1940* provides a great deal of information. There is room for a similar study of the British etchers of earlier years, many of whom, like the Norwich painters and E. W. Cooke, produced work of the highest quality. The line engravers have been poorly treated; there are many about whom little seems to be recorded apart from their names, although those who concentrated on sporting scenes have been studied in detail, notably by F. Siltzer. Many of the line engravers were also accomplished etchers; a careful examination of their work reveals what skill and artistry the best of them possessed. Similarly, the lithographers are not adequately documented, although M. Twyman's recent volume has added much to our knowledge.

Who were the leaders? In wood engraving one name stands alone: Thomas Bewick. In copper engraving, William Woollett, William Byrne, John Greig, Wilson Lowry, Samuel Middiman and John Pye must rank high; in aquatint, the names of Ackermann's experts stand out: Bluck, Stadler, Francis Jukes, R. G. Reeve, Thomas Sutherland, the Havells and William Daniell; in steel engraving the names of Thomas Lupton, Miller, W. Radclyffe, Goodall, the Findens, the Le Keux family; and in lithography, J. D. Harding, T. S. Boys and John C. Bourne. But there is a host of others, equally proficient, or nearly so; the list that follows gives only a selection of them.

Acon, R. (early 19th century) Engraver for several of Shepherd's publications

Adlard, H. (early 19th century) Engraver for a large number of county histories

Alken, S. (1750–1815) Aquatint after W. Gilpin and topographers, but mainly sporting scenes

Allen, J. B. (1803–76) Engraver on steel and wood, after Turner

Allen, J. C. (*fl* 1831) Engraver after Turner and Stanfield. Many book illustrations. Pupil of W. B. Cooke

Angus, W. (1752–1821) Engraver after Sandby and Dayes (*Seats of Nobility & Gentry*)

Apostool, C. (1762–1844) Aquatint after S. Ireland (*Wye, Thames, Medway*)

Appleton, J. W. (early 19th century) Engraver

Archer, J. W. Engraver, wood engraver and watercolourist (*Fountains Abbey*, with W. Collard)

Armytage, J. C. (1820–97) Engraver after Turner

Ashley, Alfred Etcher; author of *Art of Etching*, 1849

Baily, J. (1750–1819) Engraver, aquatint

Banks, W. (mid 19th century) Engraver (Martineau's *English Lakes*)

Barber, T. (*fl* 1835) Engraver—*Isle of Wight* and many topographical books

Barker, T. (1769–1847) Lithographer. One of the Barkers of Bath, better known as a painter

Basire, I. (1704–68) Engraver. First of four generations

Basire, J. (1730–82) Engraver. Worked for Royal Society of Antiquaries, as did his son and grandson. Blake was his apprentice

Basire, J. (1796–1869) Engraver

Batty, Lt Col R. (1789–1848) Etcher (*Welsh Scenery* 1823). Amateur draughtsman; several foreign views

Baynes, T. M. (1794–*c*1852) Lithographer (*Environs of London*)

Benjamin, E. (mid 19th century) Engraver, topographical books

Bentley, J. C. (1809–51) Engraver. Pupil of R. Brandard; worked for Fisher's and Virtue's publications, mostly after major painters

Bentley, R. E. (1788–1849) Engraver, son of above

Bewick, J. (1760–95) Wood engraver, brother of Thomas

Bewick, R. E. (1788–1849) Wood engraver, son of Thomas

Bewick, T. (1753–1828) Wood engraver. See text

Bluck, J. Aquatint for several of Ackermann's coloured publications (Holland and Barber's *Six Views in Derbyshire*, his own *Four Views* in Gloucestershire, fourteen volumes in all)

Bond, H. (mid 19th century) Engraver, topographical books

Bonner, G. W. (1796–1836) Wood engraver, and colour printer

Bourne, J. C. (1814–96) Lithographer (*London and Birmingham*, and *Great Western Railway*). See text

Boydell, John (1719–1804) Engraver, publisher. See text

Boydell, Josiah (*c*1750–1817) Engraver, publisher, nephew and partner of John

Boys, T. S. (1803–74) Lithographer (*Views of York*, 1841, *London As It Is*, 1843). See text

Bradshaw, S. (mid 19th century) Engraver, topographical books

Brandard, J. (1812–63) Engraver after Turner

Brandard, R. (1805–62) Engraver after Turner and etcher

Brannon, A. (mid 19th century) Engraver, Isle of Wight specialist

Brannon, G. (mid 19th century) Engraver (Isle of Wight views, *Vectis Scenery*, coloured aquatints)

Brannon, P. (mid 19th century) Engraver, Isle of Wight specialist

Britton, J. (1771–1857) Engraver, publisher. See text

Buck, N. Engraver, younger brother of Samuel

Buck, S. (1696–1779) Engraver (Bucks' *Views* and *Prospects*)

Buckle, D. (mid 19th century) Engraver

Buckler, J. C. (1770–1851) Engraver, aquatint (*English Cathedrals*, etc)

Burdett, P. P. (*fl* 1770) Aquatint, probably first English user of the process

Byrne, W. (1743–1805) Engraver, father of J. and Letitia (*Antiquities of Great Britain*, *Views of the Lakes*, *Britannia Depicta*). One of the best copper engravers

Calvert, E. (1800–83) Wood engraver

Calvert, F. (*fl* 1815–30) Engraver, lithographer (Harral and Ireland's *Severn*)

Carrick, R. (*fl* 1840–50) Lithographer

Cartwright, T. Aquatint (*Cambria Depicta*)

Catton, C. jnr (1756–1819) Engraver

Cave, H. (1780–1836) Etcher (*Antiquities of York*)

Chesham, F. (1749–1806) Etcher, aquatint. Engraver after Sandby and G. Robertson

Child, G. Lithographer

Clennell, L. (1781–1840) Wood engraver. Watercolour painter

Cooke, E. W. (1811–80) Etcher, engraver (*Shipping & Craft*). Also painter

Cooke, G. (1781–1834) Engraver after Turner, father of E.W.

Cooke, W. B. (1778–1853) Engraver after Turner. Worked with brother on Britton's *Beauties*, Turner's *Southern Coast*, etc

Cooke, W. J. (1797–1865) Engraver after Turner and Stanfield

Cotman, J. S. (1782–1842) Etcher. Major painter; co-founder of Norwich School

Cotman, M. E. (1810–58) Etcher, lithographer. Son of J.S.

Cousen, C. (1803–89) Engraver after Turner

Cousen, J. (1803–80) Engraver after Turner

Cox, D. (1783–59) Etcher (soft ground). Leading watercolour painter

Cox, D. jnr (1809–85) Etcher

Cozens, J. R. (1752–99) Etcher (soft ground). Major watercolour painter

Creswick, T. (1811–69) Etcher, wood engraver, painter

Crome, J. (1768–1821) Etcher (*Norfolk Picturesque Scenery*). Major painter, co-founder of Norwich School

Cuitt, G. (1779–1819) Etcher (*Wanderings . . . amongst the Ruins of Olden Times*)

Dalziel, Edward (b 1817) Wood engraver. Well known as mid 19th century book illustrator

Dalziel, George (b 1815) Wood engraver. As above

Dalziel, John (1822–69) Wood engraver. As above

Dalziel, Thomas (b 1823) Wood engraver. As above

Daniell, E. T. (1804–42) Etcher. Pupil of Crome, became London curate

Daniell, S. (1775–1811) Engraver, aquatint

Daniell, T. (1749–1840) Aquatint

Daniell, W. (1769–1837) Aquatint (*Voyage around Great Britain*, and several series of plates, including major Indian set)

Day, W. (1797–1845) Lithographer, printer and publisher

Dayes, E. (1763–1804) Engraver, mezzotint. Watercolour painter

Deeble, W. (*fl* 1815–30) Engraver, topographical books

Delamotte, W. (1775–1863) Etcher (*Thirty Etchings of Rural Subjects*, 1816). Better known as watercolourist

Dewing, H. J. (1745–1814) Etcher

Dixon, R. (1780–1815) Etcher. Norwich painter

Doo, G. T. (1800–86) Engraver, stipple

Dubourg, M. (1786–1838) Aquatint ('Gilpin's Day')

Easling, J. C. (*c*1780–1830) Mezzotint, after Turner

Edwards, W. C. (1777–1855) Engraver

Ellis, W. (1747–1810) Engraver, aquatint

Fielding, T. H. (1781–1851) Engraver, aquatint (*Descriptions of the River Wye*), painter

Finden, E. F. (1791–1857) Engraver (*Ports and Harbours*)

Finden, W. (1787–1882) Engraver (*Ports and Harbours*)

Fisher, S. (mid 19th century) Engraver, topographical books

Fittler, J. (1758–1835) Engraver, etcher (*Scotia Depicta* after Nattes)

Ford, J. (early 19th century) Aquatint

Gainsborough, T. (1727–88) Etcher, aquatint. Major painter

Gardnor, J. (1729–1808) Aquatint

Gauci, W. (*fl* 1850) Lithographer (Delamotte's *Views of Oxford*)

Geddes, A. (1783–1844) Etcher

Geikie, W. (1795–1837) Etcher, painter

Gibson, P. (1782–1829) Engraver, etcher, painter (*Etchings of Select Views in Edinburgh*, 1818)

Gilpin, W. S. Aquatint after W. Gilpin, whose brother, Sawrey, also made etchings and re-engraved later issues of plates

Girtin, T. (1775–1802) Etcher. Important watercolour painter

Glover, J. (1767–1849) Etcher, painter

Godfrey, J. (mid 19th century) Engraver, after Billings and other topographical work

Goodall, E. (1795–1870) Engraver, etcher, after Turner. Three sons and daughter all well-known painters

Gough, R. (1735–1809) Etcher

Graham, C. Lithographer

Green, W. (1761–1823) Aquatint (after J. G. Wood, *Views in Kent*), etcher (*60 small prints of the Lakes*, 1814)

Greig, J. (*fl* 1800–15) Engraver (see Storer, and Scott's *Border Antiquities* after Clennell)

Griffith, M. (1749–1809) Engraver, etcher, draughtsman for Thomas Pennant

Haghe, L. (1806–85) Lithographer

Hamble, J. (*c*1790–1824) Aquatint (Papworth's *Select Views of London*, and 'Gilpin's Day')

Harding, J. D. (1798–1863) Etcher, lithographer, engraver (*Sketches at Home and Abroad, The Park and the Forest*). Painter

Harraden, R. (1756–1858) Aquatint, and draughtsman for *Cantabrigia Depicta*, published by his father

Harvey, W. (1796–1866) Wood engraver

Hassell, J. (1767–1825) Aquatint (*Picturesque Rides and Walks, Tour of the Grand Junction, Beauties of Antiquity, Tour of Isle of Wight*). Painter. See text

Havell, D. (*fl* 1812–26) Aquatint for Ackermann's coloured publications. With brother Robert aquatinted brother William's *Thames*; also after Hassell

Havell, R. (*fl* 1812–37) Aquatint (*Noblemen's and Gentlemen's Seats*, 1814–23, W. Havell's *Thames*)

Havell, W. (1782–1857) Lithographer, painter

Hawkins, B. W. (1810–52) Lithographer

Hawkins, G. (1809–52) Lithographer. Views of Britannia and Conway bridges

Heath, C. (1785–1848) Engraver

Heath, J. (1757–1834) Engraver, publisher. Father of C.

Higham, T. (1796–1844) Engraver, after Turner, Harding and Prout. Pupil of Greig

Hill, J. (1770–1850) Aquatint (Nattes' *Views of Bath*, Ackermann's *Oxford*)

Hodgetts, T. (*c*1800–45) Mezzotint, after Turner

Hollar, W. (1607–77) Etcher. See text

Hollis, G. (*c*1790–1840) Engraver after Turner. Pupil of G. Cooke

Hollis, T. (1818–43) Engraver. Son and assistant of George Hollis

Horner, J. Lithographer (*Buildings in Halifax*, 1835)

Horsburgh, J. (1791–1869) Engraver, after Turner

Horsburgh, T. (early 19th century) Engraver

Hughes, S. G. Aquatint

Hullmandel, C. J. (1789–1850) Lithographer. See text

Ingrey, C. Lithographer (*Antiquities of Sussex*)

Ireland, S. (1725–1800) Etcher, aquatint, painter

Jackson, J. (1801–48) Wood engraver

Jeavons, T. (*c*1800–67) Engraver after Turner

Jewitt, O. S. (1799–1869) Wood engraver, etcher, aquatint

Jukes, F. (1748–1812) Aquatint, a few after W. Gilpin

Keene, C. S. (1823–91) Etcher. *Punch* illustrator

Kernot, J. (early 19th century) Engraver, after Turner

King, B. Lithographer

King, D. (*c* 1610–64) Etcher

Kip, J. (1653–1722) Etcher and engraver. See text

Ladbrooke, J. B. (1803–79) Lithographer

Ladbrooke, R. (1770–1842) Lithographer. Norwich painter

Landseer, J. (1769–1852) Engraver. Father of Sir Edwin

Landseer, T. (1795–1850) Engraver, etcher

Laporte, J. (1761–1839) Engraver, soft-ground etcher, aquatint, etched after Gainsborough

Laurie, R. (1749–1804) Print publisher, Laurie & Whittle

Le Blon, J. C. (1667–1741) Mezzotint printing in three colours

Le Blond, A. (1819–94) Engraving and colour printing, Baxter type

Le Keux, H. (1787–1868) Engraver. Brother of J.

Le Keux, J. (1783–1846) Engraver. See text

Le Keux, J. H. (1812–96) Engraver. Son of J.

Lewis, F. C. (1779–1856) Etcher, aquatint, mezzotint (*Scenery of the Dart, Tamar and Tavy, Exe*, and *Devonshire Rivers*)

Linnell, J. (1792–1852) Etcher. Best known as painter

Linton, H. D. (1815–99) Wood engraver for *Illustrated London News*

Lizars, W. H. (1788–1859) Engraver, publisher

Lodge, W. (1649–89) Etcher

Loggan, D. (1625–93) Etcher and engraver

Loutherbourg, P. de (1740–1812) Etcher, painter

Lowry, J. W. (1803–79) Engraver

Lowry, Wilson (1762–1824) Engraver. Father of J. W.

Lucas, D. (1801–81) Mezzotint, after Constable

Lupton, T. G. (1791–1873) Engraver, mezzotint, after Turner

Malton, J. (1761–1803) Engraver, aquatint

Malton, T. (1748–1804) Aquatint, draughtsman

Mazell, P. (*fl* 1760–95) Engraver, after Moses Griffith for Pennant's *Tours*, after George Smith of Chichester, and for Cordinier's *Romantic Ruins in N. Britain*, 1792

Medland, T. (1755–1822) Engraver, aquatint (Duke of Rutland's *Journal of Tours in Great Britain*)

Middiman, S. (1750–1831) Engraver (*Select Views*). See text

Miller, W. (1796–1882) Engraver, after Turner. Pupil of G. Cooke. Also watercolourist

Miln, R. (early 18th century) Engraver

Milton, T. (1743–1827) Engraver

Morris, T. (1750–1800) Engraver

Muller, W. J. (1812–45) Lithographer

Nash, F. (1782–1856) Lithographer. Best known as architectural draughtsman and watercolourist, for Ackermann's publications

Nattes, J. C. (1765–1822) Aquatint, painter

Neale, J. P. (c1771–1847) Engraver, watercolourist and draughtsman

Nesbit, C. (1775–1838) Wood engraver

Nicholson, F. (1753–1844) Lithographer, engraver, painter. Scarborough specialist (see Painters)

Nicholson, I. (1789–1848) Wood engraver

Ninham, H. (1793–1874) Etcher, lithographer, painter

Orme, E. (early 19th century) Aquatint, printseller

Palmer, S. (1805–81) Etcher, major painter

Le Petit, W. (mid 19th century) Engraver, large number of topographical books. Brother of A. Le Petit

Picken, T. (1815–70) Lithographer (Pyne's *Lake Scenery of England*)

Pickett, W. (early 19th century) Aquatint (engraved de Loutherbourg's *Picturesque Scenery of England and Wales*)

Pollard, J. (1797–1867) Mezzotint, aquatint

Prestel, Marie (1747–94) Aquatint

Prior, T. A. (1809–86) Engraver, after Turner

Prout, S. (1783–1852) Etcher, lithographer, aquatint, painter

Pyall, H. (early 19th century) Engraver, aquatint (*Coloured Views on the Liverpool and Manchester Railway*, after T. T. Bury, 1831)

Pye, C. (1777–1864) Engraver

Pye, J. (c1758–74) Engraver, etcher. Brother of C.

Pye, J. (1782–1874) Engraver, after Turner

Pyne, W. H. (1769–1843) Etcher, painter

Radclyffe, C. W. (b. 1817) Lithographer, especially Schools—Eton, Rugby, Winchester, Westminster, Shrewsbury, 1842–6 (*Pictorial Antiquities of Hereford*, c1845)

Radclyffe, E. (1809–63) Engraver, etcher, after Cox

Radclyffe, W. (1780–1855) Engraver, after Turner; for Roscoe's *North* and *South Wales* mostly after Cox

Rawle, S. (1771–1860) Engraver, after Turner

Reeve, R. G. (1803–89) Aquatint (Westall & Owen's *Thames*, Ackermann's *Cambridge*)

Reeve, T. (early 19th century) Aquatint

Reynolds, S. W. snr (1773–1835) Etcher, mezzotint, aquatint

Reynolds, S. W. jnr (1794–1872) Mezzotint

Richardson, T. M. (1813–90) Lithographer, mezzotint, painter (Newcastle-on-Tyne)

Rimmer, A. (1829–83) Wood engraver

Roberts, P. Aquatint (Calvert's *Isle of Wight*)

Roffe, J. (1769–1850) Engraver, aquatint

Rooker, E. (1711–74) Engraver, etcher

Rooker, M. (1743–1801) Engraver, etcher, painter. Son of E.

Rosenberg, C. (early 19th century) Aquatint (some plates in Raye's *Picturesque Tour through the Isle of Wight*)

Rosenberg, F. (*fl* 1828–35) Aquatint

Rosenberg, R. (early 19th century) Engraver, aquatint

Ross, J. (1745–1821) Engraver

Rowe, G. (1797–1864) Lithographer (*Illustrations of Hastings*, c1820)

Rowlandson, T. (1756–1827) Etcher (*Oxford and Cambridge*, *Sketches from Nature*), figures for Ackermann's coloured publications. Major watercolourist

Russell, J. (1745–1806) Engraver

Saddler, J. (1813–92) Engraver, after Turner

Sandby, P. (1725–1809) Aquatint, etcher, painter. See text

Sasse, R. (1774–1849) Etcher

Say, W. (1768–1834) Mezzotint, after Turner

Shepherd, T. H. (1793–1864) Aquatint, painter, London specialist

Sherlock, W. P. (1780–c1820) Engraver, etcher, draughtsman

Smith, G. (1714–76) Etcher, painter, particularly of Chichester

Smith, J. (1717–64) Etcher. Brother of G.

Smith, J. C. (1778–1816) Engraver

Smith, W. R. Engraver, after Turner

Sparrow, C. (late 18th century) Engraver

Stadler, J. C. (d 1812) Aquatint, mezzotint after de Loutherbourg, and Farington for Boydell's *Thames* and several of Ackermann's coloured publications. 31 books

Stannard, J. (1797–1830) Etcher, painter; Norwich School

Stark, J. (1794–1859) Etcher, painter; Norwich School

Storer, J. (1781–1837) Engraver (*Antiquarian and Topographical Cabinet*, with J. Greig, 1807–11, 500 plates in all)

Stothard, C. A. (1786–1821) Etcher

Stothard, T. (1755–1834) Etcher, engraver, painter

Sutherland, T. (c1785–1820) Aquatint, Ackermann's coloured publications, twenty volumes

Swan, J. Engraver (after Joseph Fleming, especially *Views of the Lakes of Scotland*, 49 plates, 1836, and *Views on the River Clyde*, 42 plates, 1830)

Thomas, W. L. (1830–1910) Wood engraver (*The Graphic*)

Thompson, C. (1791–1843) Wood engraver

Tingle, J. (*c*1830–60) Engraver, mezzotint

Tombleson, W. (*fl* 1820–40) Engraver, publisher of *Eighty Picturesque Views on the Thames and Medway*, after own paintings

Tomkins, C. (1750–1823) Etcher, aquatint (*Tour to the Isle of Wight*, 1796, many views in Reading, Malton's *Picturesque Tour through London and Westminster*, 1792–1801)

Toms, W. H. (1712–50) Engraver. Teacher of Boydell

Topham, F. W. (1808–57) Engraver, watercolourist

Turner, C. (1773–1857) Mezzotint, aquatint

Varley, C. (1781–1873) Etcher, lithographer

Varrall, J. C. (early 19th century) Engraver, after Turner

Vincent, G. (1796–1836) Etcher, mezzotint, painter; Norwich School

Vivares, F. (1709–80) Engraver, etcher

Vivares, T. (1735–1808) Engraver, soft-ground etcher. Son of F.

Walker, A. (1725–65) Engraver

Walker, J. (end 18th century) Engraver, publisher *New Copper-Plate Magazine*, 1794–6. Son of W.

Walker, W. (1729–93) Engraver. Brother of A.

Wallis, R. (1794–1878) Engraver, after Turner

Warren, C. T. (1767–1823) Engraver

Watts, W. (1752–1851) Engraver (*Seats of Nobility and Gentry*, 1779–86)

Wells, W. F. (1762–1836) Etcher, painter; etched after Gainsborough

Westall, R. (1765–1836) Engraver, soft ground etcher, aquatint; mainly painter

Westall, W. (1781–1850) Engraver, soft-ground etcher, aquatint; mainly painter

Wilkinson, J. (late 18th century) Etcher

Willmore, A. (1814–88) Engraver, soft-ground etcher

Willmore, W. T. (1800–63) Engraver, after Turner

Wing, C. W. Lithographer

Winkles, B. (early 19th century) Engraver

Winkles, H. (early 19th century) Engraver

Winkles, R. (early 19th century) Engraver

Woollett, W. (1735–85) Engraver, etcher. Worked often with F. Vivares
Woolnoth, W. (1785–c1836) Engraver
Wyld, W. (1806–98) Lithographer

SELECT BIBLIOGRAPHY

Abbey, J. R. *Scenery of Great Britain and Ireland in aquatint and lithography, from the Library of J. R. Abbey* London 1952

Ashley, A. *The Art of Etching on Copper* London 1849

Bewick, T. *A Memoir of Thomas Bewick, Written by Himself* London 1862

Britton, John. *Autobiography* London 1849

Burke, J. *English Art, 1714–1800* Oxford 1976

Chamberlain, W. *Engraving and Etching* London 1972

Fielding, T. H. *The Art of Engraving* London 1841

Godfrey, R. T. *Printmaking in Britain* Oxford 1978

Grant, M. H. *Dictionary of Etchers* London 1952

Graves, A. *Dictionary of Artists* London 1891 (reprinted in facsimile, Bath 1969)

Gray, Basil. *The English Print* London 1937

Grigson, G. *Britain Observed* London 1975

Gross, A. *Etching, Engraving and Intaglio Printing* London 1973

Guichard, K. M. *British Etchers, 1850–1940* London 1977

Hamerton, P. G. *Etching and Etchers* London 1868

Hardie, M. *English Coloured Books* London 1906

—— *Water Colour Painting in Britain* London 1966–8

Hayden, A. *Chats on Old Prints* London 1900

Hind, A. M. *A History of Engraving and Etching* London 1908

Holloway, M. *A Bibliography of Nineteenth Century British Topographical Books with Steel Engravings* London 1977

Irwin, D. and F. *Scottish Painters* London 1975

Ivins, W. *Prints and Visual Communication* Cambridge, Mass 1953

Klingender, F. G. *Art and the Industrial Revolution* London 1968

London Directory, The 1791

Maxted, I. *The London Book Trades, 1775–1800*

Parris, L. *Landscape in Britain, c1750–1850* London 1973. The catalogue of a Tate Gallery exhibition

Phillips, J. F. C. *Shepherd's London* London 1976

Plant, M. *The English Book Trade* London 1974

Prideaux, S. T. *Aquatint Engraving* London 1909

Rawlinson, W. *Turner's Liber Studiorum* London 1906

—— *The Engraved Work of J. M. W. Turner* London 1908

Redgrave, R. *Dictionary of Artists of the English School* London 1878

Roget, J. L. *History of the Old Water Colour Society* London 1891

Sandby, W. *Thomas and Paul Sandby* London 1892

Slythe, R. M. *The Art of Illustration* London 1970

Somers Cocks, J. V. *Devonshire Topographical Prints 1660–1870* Exeter 1977

Tooley, R. V. *English Colour Plate Books* London 1954

Twyman, M. *Lithography 1800–1850. The techniques of drawing on stone in England and France and their application in works of topography* London 1970

Vaughan, J. *The English Guide Book* Newton Abbot 1974

Weinreb & Douwma, Ltd. *Catalogues 17 and 19* 1977–8

Whitman, A. *The Print Collector's Handbook* (reprinted Wakefield 1973 from the 1907 ed)

Wilton, A. *British Watercolours, 1750–1850* Oxford 1977

ACKNOWLEDGEMENTS

I am grateful to many people for their help and advice, including several print dealers and antiquarian booksellers. The late Miss C. Jelf, Maggy Ross, Sue Lambert of the Victoria and Albert Museum, Judy Hines of Norwich, Hilary Chapman, and R. F. O'Shea of Baynton-Williams all gave help when it was needed. I am especially indebted to Brian Stevens of Monmouth who provided the original inspiration and gave much advice and assistance in the early stages of the project.

Plates 3, 8, 17, 33 and 48 are from the Victoria and Albert Museum; 15, 19, 20, 35, 37 and 38 from the Cambridge University Library; 16 from Newmarket Gallery; 18, 39 and 41 from B. J. Stevens, Church St, Monmouth. The remainder belong to my own collection.

To my wife, Jill, for finding me the time in which to write, I am always grateful.

INDEX